The Dead Don't Need Stuff

Declutter Your Life

Richard Lowe

The Writing King

The Dead Don't Need Stuff: Declutter Your Life

Disclaimer

This book contains personal accounts of family dysfunction, hoarding behavior, depression, and difficult relationships. Some of these experiences involve emotional abuse and trauma. The author shares these stories to provide authentic context for the decluttering methods described, not as a substitute for professional mental health support.

The Emotional Audit method described in Chapter 2 is a practical tool developed through personal experience. It is not a therapeutic technique, and this book is not a substitute for therapy or professional mental health care. If the process of going through your belongings surfaces significant emotional pain, grief, or trauma responses, please consider working with a qualified mental health professional alongside this work. There is no shame in needing support. Some of us are carrying more than a junk drawer.

It is also worth acknowledging that some people are not yet ready to begin this process at all. If your accumulation is deeply tied to trauma, grief, or mental health conditions that have not been addressed, a decluttering book is not the right first step. Therapy is. There is no shame in that sequence. Get the support you need first. This book will still be here.

The names of certain family members and individuals in this book have been used with the understanding that they are now deceased. Some identifying details of people outside the immediate family have been changed or omitted to protect their privacy.

The author is not a therapist, psychologist, licensed counselor, or mental health professional of any kind. He is a person who grew up in a hoarding household, spent years replicating the patterns he observed, and eventually figured out how to stop. Everything in this book comes from that experience, not from a clinical credential.

Table of Contents

Prologue: The Rose Parade Pins That Saved My Sanity

I was sitting at my kitchen table with a pair of scissors in one hand and four sets of Tournament of Roses pins in the other, about to cut apart something I'd collected for years, when I realized I'd lost my mind.

This was decluttering phase number seven for me, and I was deep in that dangerous zone where you stop thinking and start purging everything in sight. The pins were beautiful: four complete sets of fifty pins each from different years of the Rose Parade, carefully mounted and displayed. But I was in full declutter mode, and in that state, everything looks like clutter.

"I could sell these individually on eBay," I told myself, already planning how to photograph each pin separately, write individual descriptions, calculate shipping costs. "Fifty pins times four sets, that's two hundred listings."

Before I started cutting, something made me check eBay first. Good thing, because similar pins were selling for maybe two or three dollars each. After eBay's fees, I'd make perhaps a dollar per pin. Two hundred hours of work for two hundred dollars, destroying something I liked in the process.

I put the scissors down and looked at those pin sets with fresh eyes. They weren't clutter. They were a collection I enjoyed, representing years of attending the Rose Parade, memories of New Year's Days spent watching the floats roll by. I was about to destroy something meaningful because I'd gotten caught up in purge momentum.

I'd been here before. Seven times.

This wasn't my first decluttering rodeo. Seven major purges of my possessions, each one triggered by different circumstances, each one teaching me something different about the relationship between people and their stuff. Some of those purges were necessary for my emotional survival. Others nearly destroyed things I valued because I couldn't tell the difference between clutter and collections.

I'm not a hoarder. I'm a collector. Most decluttering advice misses this crucial difference completely.

Hoarders keep everything because they can't make decisions about what to let go. Collectors keep specific things because those things matter to them. The problem comes when collectors get overwhelmed by the sheer volume of their interests and decide to purge everything, throwing away the valuable collections along with the actual clutter.

I've collected stamps since I was twelve. At one point, I had thousands of them, taking up an entire wall of albums. During one of my earlier purges, I got rid of about eighty percent of them. But when I picked up my Tonga stamps and my Disney collection, I stopped cold. Those weren't clutter. Those were the stamps I cared about, the ones that brought me joy when I looked at them. The rest were just accumulation.

My books were the same story. Thousands of paperbacks and pulp magazines, stacked three deep on rickety shelves that were becoming a fire hazard. Most of them had served their purpose: I'd read them once and would never read them again. But scattered throughout that chaos were books I referenced, authors I loved, and vintage pulps that connected me to the history of science fiction. Learning to distinguish between books I owned and books I treasured took several purges to figure out.

The first time I sold stuff on eBay, I made thirty-five thousand dollars. That's not a typo. I had accumulated an enormous amount of valuable items, and when I finally started selling, the money was substantial. Each subsequent purge has yielded less, partly because I'd already sold the obviously valuable stuff, and partly because eBay's fees have gotten so ridiculous that it's barely worth the effort anymore.

The real point was reclaiming my space and my sanity from the tyranny of too much stuff.

Not every purge was about collections and hobbies. After my wife passed away, I did a completely different kind of decluttering. I filled an entire trash bin with medical equipment, medications, and painful reminders that I needed gone from my daily environment to survive my grief. I also got rid of everything that belonged to my father, whom I'd been estranged from since I moved out in 1981 — nearly forty years. But the objects had stayed: his artwork, early drawings from his Air Force and civil service career, childhood gifts. That purge felt different from the collection purges. It wasn't grief exactly. It was release.

Those seven phases taught me: there's a time to purge and a time to stop. There's a difference between clutter that weighs you down and collections that bring you joy. There's a distinction between keeping things out of fear and keeping things out of love.

Most decluttering advice treats all possessions as equally suspicious, as if the goal is to own as little as possible. That's not realistic for people who have genuine interests and passions. The goal isn't to become a monk living in an empty room. The goal is to keep what serves your life and let go of what doesn't.

I learned this the hard way, by almost destroying things I valued because I couldn't tell the difference between momentum and wisdom. Those Rose Parade pins sitting safely in their display case remind me every day that decluttering is as much about knowing when to stop as it is about knowing when to start.

The pins story isn't the exception to this book's advice. It is the advice.

Knowing what to keep is the harder skill. Any idiot can throw everything away. What takes judgment is looking at something and being honest about whether it belongs in your life — whether it's genuinely yours or just accumulated — and acting on that difference. That's what I learned with those pins. Not "keep everything." Not "get rid of everything." Keep what's actually yours. Let go of what isn't.

That distinction is what the rest of this book is about.

Introduction: Welcome to Clutter Anonymous

Hi, my name is Richard, and I caught myself before it was too late.

My parents Jerry and Valerie were hoarders. By the time they died, they had a one-bedroom apartment packed floor-to-ceiling with pathways and two storage units crammed full of "valuable" stuff they never saw again. I recognized the pattern early, saw where it was heading, and executed several massive decluttering campaigns that probably saved my sanity, my relationships, and quite possibly my life.

Growing up in a family where accumulating things was a competitive sport gives you a unique perspective on clutter. My mother had severe depression, and my father discovered early that buying her things provided temporary relief. A new antique, a kitchen gadget, something shiny and new would calm her down for a little while. So he kept buying. I watched this dynamic as a small child without understanding it, and after I moved out, I replicated it. When my own depression hit, I spent vast sums on junk thinking it would help. It didn't. It made things worse.

My parents weren't always clinical hoarders. Valerie started collecting antiques and knick-knacks with some organization to it. Jerry collected art supplies, which made sense for someone who worked as a graphics artist and later as a self-employed painter. My maternal grandmother Jean collected UFO magazines and books with the dedication of someone who believed the information might actually matter someday.

Somewhere along the way, collecting became accumulating, and accumulating became hoarding. Valerie's antiques multiplied into everything remotely old or "interesting." Jerry's art supplies evolved into saving every piece of everything that might ever be valuable. Jean's UFO magazines expanded to include every publication about obscure practices she could lay her hands on.

When Claudia died in 2005, I was surrounded by evidence of what I was becoming. Her things, my things, a household full of accumulated weight — and suddenly all of it was just mine to deal with. I spent a year pitching her belongings into garbage bins as a form of survival. In that year, I read a book called Not for Packrats Only, and it landed exactly right. I looked around at what I'd built up and recognized the pattern. I was heading down the exact same path as my parents.

I told myself I was different. I was a "collector," not a hoarder. I had interests, hobbies, legitimate reasons for acquiring things. But when I looked at my accumulated stuff, I saw the warning signs everywhere. Books I'd never read again taking up entire walls. CDs I'd never listen to now that everything was digital. Clothes that fit the person I used to be, not the person I am. Kitchen gadgets that seemed essential at the store but had been used exactly once before being banished to a drawer.

If I didn't do something drastic, I was going to end up exactly where they did: surrounded by so much stuff that I couldn't live my life.

So I did something they never managed to do: I learned to tell the difference between what mattered and what didn't, and I acted on that difference.

Years later, when my parents died, they had managed to fill three separate locations with stuff: a one-bedroom apartment where you had to follow narrow pathways between towers of belongings, plus two storage units they were paying monthly rent on to house items they couldn't even access. After my mother died, my father donated the contents of one storage unit. Then he died too. I was 3,000 miles away. I got a call from the social worker who managed the apartment complex describing the scene. She wanted to know what to do with everything. I told her to donate it all.

I felt numb. Not surprised — I'd watched the accumulation build for decades. Not triumphant — they were gone. Just numb, and quietly aware that I'd already made different choices.

For several years, I executed what I now call "massive decluttering campaigns." These weren't gentle, Marie Kondo-style "does it spark joy" sessions. These were full-scale military operations against my possessions. I didn't just organize my stuff. I got rid of a lot of it. I sold it on eBay, donated it, gave it away, and yes, threw a lot of it in the trash where it probably belonged in the first place.

You know what happened? I didn't miss most of it. Yes, there are a few things like the original Dungeons and Dragons rules I wish I hadn't sold, but I'd never even played the game anyway. I felt lighter, happier, and more in control of my life than I had in years. It was like I'd been carrying an invisible backpack full of rocks and finally figured out I could just take it off.

The pattern I'd absorbed as a child was subtle and destructive. I once got a specialized shopping mall gift card and spent the entire $2,000 balance on board games. I'm an introvert, but I thought if I had enough games, I'd have a reason to invite people over, and that would solve the loneliness. A full closet of board games. They collected dust for a decade. I eventually threw out all of them except a couple I genuinely liked. The buying didn't solve the problem. It created new ones: debt, a full moving van worth of junk to haul every time I relocated, and more depression because the things I'd bought to feel better were now weighing me down. It was a spiral. Recognizing it as a spiral was the only way out.

What I didn't understand at the time was that the buying wasn't just failing to help — it was adding to the problem. Every object acquired during a depressive episode carried that episode with it. The board games sat in the closet not just taking up space but carrying the specific loneliness and desperation of the night I bought them. A $4,000 camera setup I rarely used carried the anxiety that drove the purchase. Computers I'd replaced but kept carried the insecurity of thinking I might need to go back. I was filling my home with emotional weight while trying to feel lighter. The solution and the problem were the same thing.

Here's what I eventually understood: I wasn't weighed down by all my junk. I was weighed down by the negative emotions and memories attached to specific objects. Getting rid of those objects wasn't tidying up. It was closer to light therapy. Every time I walked past something connected to a harmful relationship or a painful period, some part of my brain registered the damage. Multiply that across a houseful of negatively charged objects and you're living in a constant low hum of bad feeling without even realizing it. Remove those objects and the hum stops.

Nobody tells you this about decluttering: it's not really about the stuff. It's about understanding why the stuff accumulated in the first place. For some people it's depression. For some it's anxiety about scarcity. For some it's identity — surrounding yourself with objects that tell you who you are. Until you see the real reason, the practical advice in every decluttering book in existence won't stick.

This book will teach you how to get rid of the clutter. But more importantly, it will help you understand why it's there. I'll show you the practical methods — the four piles, the emergency purge, the room-by-room approach — but I'll also show you the psychology underneath it. Because without that, you'll declutter once and be back where you started within a year.

I'm going to share the real stories from my family's journey because sometimes the best way to avoid a destination is to see exactly where that road leads. You'll meet the people in this story: Valerie with her antiques and knick-knack archives, driven by depression my father enabled by buying her things. Jerry with his art supplies and outdoor gear and garage full of equipment for activities that happened once or never. Jean, my maternal grandmother, with her own milder version of the same pattern. And me — the kid who watched all of it, told himself he was a collector not a hoarder, and spent the next thirty years proving himself wrong.

One thing you'll notice as you go through this process: the clutter in your home has patterns. It's not random. The same categories show up in the same places for reasons that reflect how you actually live and what your specific psychological relationship with accumulation looks like.

Some people have a clothing problem — closets and dressers packed to capacity, clothes that haven't been worn in years, shopping that happened in bursts during difficult periods. Some people have a paper problem — mail, documents, receipts, magazines, things that were going to be filed or read or dealt with and never were. Some people have a kitchen problem — gadgets, multiples, expired food, the archaeology of cooking ambitions. Some people have a sentimental problem — objects they can't let go of because getting rid of them feels like betrayal.

Most people have a combination. And almost everyone has at least one category where the accumulation is significantly worse than the rest, because that category is where their particular psychology operates most strongly.

Identifying your pattern early makes the work faster. If you know your kitchen is your worst area, you start there and build momentum in the place where you'll see the most dramatic results. If you know sentimental items are your sticking point, you know to address the emotional component before you tackle the boxes in the closet, not to stand in front of them hoping for sudden clarity.

Pay attention as you go through the chapters ahead. Notice which sections make you uncomfortable, which examples hit close to home, which categories you're already telling yourself won't be that bad. The ones you're least looking forward to are probably the ones you most need to address.

We'll talk about the psychology of stuff and why our brains trick us into keeping things that make our lives worse. We'll cover the practical aspects of decluttering, from the emergency purge of potentially life-ruining items to the long-term maintenance of a sane living space. We'll even tackle digital hoarding, because apparently our phones and computers can become just as cluttered as our closets.

Mostly, we're going to have some fun with this. If you can't laugh at the absurdity of paying monthly rent to store broken appliances you'll never fix or keeping clothes that fit you in high school "just in case," or saving every greeting card you've ever received as if Hallmark cards were legal documents, then you're taking this whole thing way too seriously.

The dead people in the title? They're not just my parents. They're everyone who came before us, whose stuff we inherit and feel obligated to keep forever. They're the guilt-inducing voices in our heads that say we can't throw out Great Aunt Martha's china or Grandpa's tools or Mom's collection of ceramic cats. Here's a revolutionary thought: dead people don't need their stuff. They're done with it. They've moved on. Maybe we should too.

Welcome to Clutter Anonymous, where the first step is admitting you have a problem, and the last step is discovering you can live without most of your possessions and be happier for it. We're going to declutter your space, your mind, and maybe even your family relationships, one item at a time.

Life is too short to spend it managing stuff you don't need, moving around objects that don't serve you, and feeling guilty about possessions that possess you right back.

Let's get started.

One thing this book is not going to ask you to do: get rid of everything.

That's not the goal and it's not good advice. The goal is to keep what genuinely matters to you and let go of what doesn't. That sounds simple. In practice it's harder than the scorched-earth approach, because it requires you to be honest about the difference — to look at each thing you own and ask whether it's actually earning its place in your life, or whether it's there through inertia, obligation, guilt, or the accumulated momentum of never having decided otherwise.

The decluttering books that tell you to get rid of everything, keep only essentials, own fewer than a hundred items — those books are solving a different problem than the one most people have. Most people don't need to become minimalists. They need to become discerning. Keep the stamps you love. Keep the books you actually read. Keep the tools you use and the clothes that fit and the objects that represent something real about who you are. Let go of the rest — not because owning things is bad, but because owning things you don't care about is costing you something every day.

What actually works, in brief, before the longer explanation that follows:

Starting small works. The junk drawer, not the garage. Fifteen minutes, not a whole weekend. The resistance drops after the first completed session, not before.

Understanding the psychology first works. Every chapter of this book that addresses practical methods is more effective if you've read the chapters on why accumulation happens. The methods are tools. The psychology explains when and why to use them.

Maintenance works. A decluttered home that isn't maintained returns to its previous state within a year. The people who stay clear are the ones who treat it as an ongoing practice, not a one-time project.

Honesty works. Not the brutal kind that makes you feel bad about everything you've kept. The kind that asks, without judgment, whether each thing you own is actually serving your life. Honest assessment, applied consistently, does more work than any system or method.

What doesn't work: trying to do everything at once, planning indefinitely without starting, and treating the before-and-after transformation as the goal. The transformation is a side effect of the practice. Focus on the practice.

One last thing before you dive in.

This process is going to surface some feelings you might not be expecting. Not just the practical resistance of not wanting to let things go, but sometimes genuine emotion — grief for people you've lost, regret about purchases or choices, discomfort about periods of your life you'd rather not revisit. Objects carry more than their physical weight, and going through them is a more personal process than it might appear from the outside.

This is normal. It's not a sign that you're doing it wrong or that you're too emotionally fragile for this work. It's a sign that the things you own have been with you through real experiences, and acknowledging that honestly is part of doing this well.

The practical advice: don't try to process the emotional content while you're in the middle of sorting. If something surfaces a strong feeling, note it, set the object aside in the Decide Later pile, and come back to it when you're not in the middle of a session. The combination of decision fatigue and unexpected emotion is a reliable recipe for either keeping things you should let go of or letting go of things you'll regret.

Give yourself more time than you think you need. More sessions than you plan for. More grace than you'd extend to anyone else doing this work.

You're not cleaning a house. You're making sense of a life. That takes as long as it takes.

A quick map of what's ahead.

Chapter 1 covers the psychology — why accumulation happens, what it's actually costing you, and the distinction between clutter and collections that the rest of the book depends on. Chapter 2 covers decluttering methods, including the one I developed over years of doing this for myself and helping others do it. Chapters 3 through 6 are the practical framework: the four-pile sorting system, the emergency purge of genuinely dangerous items, the twenty excuses you'll make and why they're all wrong, and the master plan for executing the whole project without burning out.

Chapters 7 through 9 cover the specific battlegrounds: every room in your house, the psychology of letting go when the practical approaches aren't enough, and the digital dimension that most decluttering books ignore entirely. Chapter 10 covers maintenance — how to keep it cleared after you've done the work. Chapter 11 covers what life actually looks like on the other side.

The Conclusion addresses the question that underlies everything: what do you want your possessions to say about you when you're not around to explain them?

You don't have to read it in order, but the chapters build on each other. The psychology in the early chapters makes the practical work in the middle chapters easier. The practical work makes the maintenance in the later chapters automatic. Start at the beginning.

There's a question worth sitting with before you start: what do you actually want from this?

Not what you think you should want. Not the before-and-after transformation Instagram has trained you to expect. What specifically would be different about your daily life if your home worked better?

For some people it's finding things. The chronic inability to locate what you need when you need it — the keys, the charger, the document — is a constant low-grade frustration that a decluttered, organized home eliminates. For some people it's having guests over without anxiety. For some people it's reclaiming a specific space — the spare room, the garage, the basement — for actual use. For some people it's the financial cost of storage or duplicates. For some people it's purely psychological: the feeling of weight that a cluttered environment creates, the sense of being managed by your possessions rather than managing them.

Knowing your specific answer focuses the work. When you get tired or frustrated partway through — and you will, because this is real work — the answer to this question is what keeps you going. Not abstract principles about simplicity, but the concrete thing you're working toward.

Write it down if that helps. What specifically changes when you're done? Keep that answer somewhere you'll see it.

You'll meet my parents in these pages — Jerry and Valerie — who accumulated their way from a functioning home to a subsidized apartment nobody knew about, with two storage units of overflow they were paying rent on until they died. I watched this happen over decades. It didn't feel like a crisis in progress. It felt like normal family life, punctuated by periods when there was noticeably more stuff than before.

That's the thing about hoarding at the family level — it normalizes itself. The house that seems crowded to a visitor seems fine to the people who live in it, because they adjusted to each new addition one at a time. You stop seeing the clutter the way you stop hearing the traffic if you live near a highway. It's just the environment.

I absorbed patterns from that environment that took me years to recognize and longer to change. The buying-as-comfort loop. The keeping-everything-just-in-case reflex. The conviction that more stuff equaled more security. These weren't conscious choices. They were the water I grew up swimming in.

This isn't a book about blaming parents or processing family dysfunction. It's a book about recognizing patterns, understanding where they come from, and making different choices. My parents' story is in here because it's the clearest illustration I have of where the road leads. Not because I want you to feel sorry for them or for me, but because the destination is useful information when you're deciding which direction to walk.

A word about resistance, because you're going to feel it.

Resistance is the force that keeps things exactly as they are. It shows up as procrastination — not today, maybe this weekend, definitely next month. It shows up as perfectionism — I can't start until I have the right system, the right containers, the right amount of uninterrupted time. It shows up as overwhelm — there's too much, I don't know where to start, this is impossible.

None of these feelings are unique to you. Every person who has successfully decluttered felt all of them. The difference between people who get through it and people who don't isn't the absence of resistance. It's the decision to start anyway, with full knowledge that the conditions will never be perfect and the time will never be ideal.

The single most effective response to resistance is also the simplest: start with something so small that resistance can't find purchase on it. Not the garage. Not the closet. The junk drawer.

Fifteen minutes. Set a timer so you know there's an end. When the timer goes off, stop. Do it again tomorrow.

The momentum builds faster than you expect. The first session is the hardest. The second is easier. By the fifth, the resistance has substantially reduced because you've accumulated evidence that this is manageable, that you don't spiral into regret, that the things you let go of don't come back to haunt you.

The title of this book is a provocation, not a eulogy.

Dead people don't need stuff. You're not dead. You're alive, and you have a life to live — and that life is being quietly consumed by the management demands of things you've accumulated without much intention and haven't been able to let go of without even more intention. The time you spend cleaning around things you don't care about, searching through piles for things you actually need, maintaining spaces that are more storage than living — that's time you could be spending on the actual content of your life.

This isn't about preparing for death. It's about not letting your stuff make your living years smaller than they need to be. Every drawer you can't close, every room you avoid, every weekend project that's actually just reorganizing accumulated junk — that's your life, being spent on stuff instead of on the things that matter to you.

Dead people don't need stuff because they're finished. You aren't. The question this book keeps asking is: what are you doing with the time and space and attention that your stuff is currently taking up?

There's a particular kind of clutter that accumulates in every home regardless of income, personality, or good intentions. Not hoarder-level catastrophe — most people reading this aren't hoarders. Just the ordinary accumulation of a life lived in a consumer culture that is very good at selling things and very bad at helping you figure out what to do with them once they stop being useful.

Maybe your garage has become a museum of abandoned hobbies. Maybe your closet is so packed you can't find anything, and you keep buying duplicates of things you already own somewhere in there. Maybe you have boxes from your last move that you haven't opened in two years. Maybe a deceased relative's belongings are sitting in storage, costing you money every month, because you haven't been able to face going through them.

None of this makes you a bad person. It makes you a person who lives in the modern world.

The modern world is extraordinarily good at creating clutter. Every purchase comes with packaging. Every hobby comes with equipment. Every phase of life leaves behind artifacts of the person you were during it. Every relationship ends with objects that carry emotional weight. And underlying all of it, a consumer culture that has spent decades perfecting the art of making you feel like buying more things will solve problems that more things cannot solve.

This book is about recognizing that cycle and interrupting it.

What you'll find here is different from most decluttering advice in one important way: we're going to deal with the psychology before we deal with the stuff. There's a reason every previous attempt you've made to get organized didn't stick. It's not that you lacked willpower or the right storage system. It's that the accumulation had reasons — emotional, psychological, habitual reasons — and sorting through physical objects without addressing those reasons just delays the next accumulation.

You're going to meet some people in these pages. Friends of mine at various stages of their own decluttering — some who got through it, some who stalled, some who found the process revealed things about their lives they hadn't expected. Their stories aren't here to make you feel better or worse about your own situation. They're here because the problems they ran into are the problems most people run into, and seeing how someone else navigated them is often more useful than abstract advice.

You're also going to find practical systems that actually work: a method for categorizing everything you own, an emergency checklist for items that could cause you serious problems if the wrong person found them, a room-by-room approach to the physical work, and maintenance habits that prevent the whole thing from quietly coming back.

The goal isn't a minimalist showroom. The goal is a home that works for the life you're actually living — not the life you used to live, not the life you think you should be living, not the life you're planning to live someday. The one you're living right now.

That's achievable. People do it every day. And the version of it that lasts isn't the dramatic weekend transformation you've probably tried before. It's a quieter, more honest process of figuring out what actually belongs in your life and letting the rest go.

Chapter 1: The Psychology of Stuff (Or: Why We're All Crazy)

Let me tell you about the day I realized my family was completely insane about objects.

I was about twelve, helping my mom Valerie rearrange her antique collection for the third time that month. She had this brass candlestick she'd moved from the mantelpiece to the bookshelf to the dining room table and back to the mantelpiece, like she was playing the world's most boring shell game. I asked her why she kept moving it around.

"Well," she said, polishing it for the hundredth time, "I want to make sure it's in the perfect spot where I can really appreciate it."

I looked around our living room, packed with more antiques than most museums, and said, "Mom, you have so many antiques you can't see any of them anymore."

She gave me that look parents give kids when they've said something profound and disturbing. Then she went back to polishing the candlestick.

That's when I first understood that my family didn't just own stuff. The stuff owned them. My dad had a garage full of outdoor equipment for activities he never did, art supplies for paintings he never finished, and every issue of National Geographic ever published piled floor to ceiling in what used to be my bedroom. My grandmother Jean had filing cabinets of UFO research she was convinced would matter when the aliens arrived. None of them saw any of this as a problem. The accumulation had become normal.

I started noticing the same pattern everywhere — neighbors with garages full of tools who called a handyman for every repair, relatives with enough books to stock a library who watched television every night instead of reading. People all around me were using objects to solve psychological problems that objects couldn't solve.

It took me years to understand what I was actually seeing. This chapter is the shortcut.

Why Your Brain Loves Clutter

Here's something nobody tells you at the start of a decluttering project: your brain is not on your side.

The human brain evolved over hundreds of thousands of years in conditions of scarcity. For most of human history, acquiring resources and holding onto them was a survival strategy. The people who kept things — tools, food, materials — were more likely to survive lean periods than the people who didn't. That instinct is baked into your nervous system at a level that logic can't easily override.

The problem is that your brain hasn't updated its operating system to account for the fact that you live in an era of unprecedented abundance. You're not going to starve because you donated a box of kitchen gadgets. The hardware store is two miles away if you need a screwdriver. And yet your brain still sends the same "hold onto this, you might need it" signal it sent to your ancestors on the savanna.

This is why decluttering feels wrong even when you know it's right. It's not weakness. It's not disorganization. It's a mismatch between an ancient survival instinct and a modern environment that's flooded with stuff.

Understanding this changes the way you approach the problem. You're not fighting laziness. You're overriding a deeply wired biological response. That requires more than motivation — it requires a different kind of thinking.

The Identity Trap

I had a friend named Darnell, a software engineer, who had a second bedroom he hadn't been able to enter in three years. The room contained kayaks, rock climbing gear, a full backpacking setup, trail running shoes in four different sizes because he kept buying them thinking the right pair would finally motivate him, and enough technical outdoor clothing to outfit a small expedition.

In five years of friendship, I never once saw Darnell do any of these activities.

When I finally asked him about the room, he said, "I'm an outdoor person. I just haven't had time lately." Lately was apparently three years and counting. The gear wasn't being used. It wasn't even accessible. It was just there, expressing the identity he wanted without requiring him to actually live it.

What struck me was how much energy he spent defending it. The kayaks especially. He'd paid serious money for them and couldn't let go of the idea that they represented something real about who he was. When I pointed out that the kayaks hadn't been on water since he bought them, he got genuinely irritated — not because I was wrong, but because I was right in a way that was uncomfortable.

Eventually he donated almost everything. He kept one good backpack and a pair of hiking boots. He started actually hiking. The identity became real only after the props were gone.

The aspirational equipment hadn't been preserving his potential. It had been substituting for it.

The most powerful psychological force driving accumulation isn't the survival instinct. It's something more subtle and more damaging: the use of objects to construct and communicate an identity.

Think about what your stuff says about you. Or rather, what you want it to say about you.

The cookbooks on your shelf suggest you're the kind of person who cooks interesting meals. The exercise equipment in the corner suggests you're the kind of person who works out. The half-finished art supplies in the closet suggest you're the kind of person who creates things. The stack of serious books on the nightstand suggests you're the kind of person who reads serious books.

Whether or not any of these things are actually true about you right now is a separate question. The objects are doing the work of projecting an identity you aspire to — or once aspired to — regardless of whether your actual daily behavior supports it.

This is the identity trap. You buy the running shoes because buying them feels like becoming a runner. You keep the guitar because keeping it feels like remaining a musician. You hold onto the foreign language textbooks because they preserve the possibility of the version of you who someday learns French.

The objects aren't just things. They're investments in a self-image. And getting rid of them feels like abandoning that self-image — which is why it triggers something that feels almost like grief.

The cruelest part is that these aspirational objects actively work against the identity they're supposed to support. Every time you walk past the guitar you're not playing, some part of your brain registers the gap between who you think you should be and who you actually are. Every unused cookbook is a small, daily reminder that you're not the person you intended to be when you bought it. The objects meant to represent your better self become a constant source of low-level guilt.

Ask yourself honestly: how many things in your home represent who you are, and how many represent who you thought you'd be or who you think you should be? For most people, it's a revealing exercise. A significant portion of what's cluttering your space is what you might call aspirational furniture — objects furnishing a life you're not actually living.

The Normalization Problem

There's another mechanism that makes clutter so hard to recognize and address: normalization.

Clutter rarely arrives all at once. It accumulates one completely reasonable acquisition at a time. The kitchen gadget that seemed genuinely useful at the store. The book that looked interesting in the moment. The box of old clothes you were definitely going to sort through. Each individual item makes sense in isolation. The problem is that each one shifts your baseline slightly — what counts as "normal" for how much stuff you have quietly adjusts upward.

This is why hoarders almost never see their situation clearly. The person living in a house where pathways thread between floor-to-ceiling stacks didn't wake up one day and decide to live that way. It happened gradually, with each addition feeling marginal, reasonable, and temporary. The accumulation is invisible because it happened incrementally.

You probably don't have a clinical hoarding situation. But the same mechanism operates at every level of accumulation. Your current normal — whatever it is — was set by years of incremental additions. The question isn't whether you have more than you once did. The question is whether your current baseline is actually serving you.

One useful exercise: walk through your home and look at everything as if you'd never seen it before. Not with your normal eyes, which have long since stopped registering half of what's there, but with the eyes of someone encountering your space for the first time. What would a stranger think about the person who lives here? What story does the accumulation tell?

Most people find this genuinely surprising. Things that had become invisible — the pile on the counter, the overflowing closet, the boxes stacked in the corner — suddenly become visible again. That visibility is the first step.

Objects as Emotional Regulation

A third psychological mechanism runs beneath the identity trap and the normalization problem, and it's the one that's hardest to address because it's the most intimate.

Many people use shopping and acquiring objects as a form of emotional regulation. When you're anxious, buying something provides a brief sense of control. When you're depressed, a new purchase offers a temporary lift. When you're bored, shopping fills the time. When you're grieving or stressed, surrounding yourself with new things creates the sensation of forward motion even when nothing is actually moving forward.

This isn't a character flaw. It's a coping mechanism, and like most coping mechanisms it works in the short term well enough to get reinforced. The problem is that it generates its own complications. The objects acquired during emotional low points carry those emotional states with them. The things you bought when you were depressed, anxious, or lonely become associated with those states. They don't just take up physical space — they occupy emotional space too.

And then you keep them, because getting rid of them requires revisiting whatever drove the purchase in the first place.

The result is a home that's not just physically cluttered but emotionally cluttered — filled with objects carrying the residue of difficult periods, unresolved feelings, and abandoned attempts to feel better through buying.

This is why standard decluttering advice often doesn't stick. "Just get rid of stuff you don't use" is easy to say and hard to do when the stuff you don't use is tangled up with grief, anxiety, loneliness, or old versions of yourself you haven't fully let go of yet. The practical advice needs the psychological foundation, or it's just rearranging the surface.

Here's the calculation most people never make: what is your stuff actually costing you in terms of your life?

Not money, though the financial cost is real. Time. The time spent managing, cleaning around, searching through, and maintaining things you don't use or care about is time spent not doing something else. The hour you spend looking for something in a cluttered space is an hour you didn't spend on a walk, on a project you care about, with someone you love, doing literally anything that matters to you.

The cognitive load compounds this. Every object in your environment that represents an unresolved decision is running in the background of your mind, consuming attention that could go somewhere else. A cluttered home isn't just visually overwhelming. It's mentally exhausting. You can't think as clearly, work as effectively, or relax as fully in a space full of things that need to be dealt with.

Dead people don't need stuff because they're not living anymore. You are. The question is whether you want to spend your living years managing accumulation or actually using them.

What Your Stuff Is Actually Costing You

Let's talk about cost in the most direct terms.

Every object you own requires maintenance attention from your brain. Not conscious attention necessarily — you're not sitting around thinking about your junk drawer — but background attention. The awareness that things need to be sorted, organized, repaired, or dealt with creates a constant low-level cognitive load. Psychologists call this the Zeigarnik effect: unfinished tasks keep running in the background of your mind, consuming resources, even when you're not consciously thinking about them.

A cluttered home is a collection of unfinished tasks. Every pile is something that hasn't been dealt with. Every broken object is a repair that hasn't happened. Every box of "stuff to sort through someday" is an open loop running in the background. Multiply that across an entire household and you're carrying a substantial cognitive burden without even realizing it.

Research on clutter and psychological wellbeing consistently finds that people in cluttered environments report higher levels of cortisol — the stress hormone — throughout the day. They report more difficulty concentrating, more fatigue, more feelings of being overwhelmed. They sleep less well. They're less productive. They feel less happy in their own homes.

The cost isn't just psychological. There's the financial cost of storage — whether you're renting units or simply paying for a larger home than you need to house your accumulation. There's the time cost of managing, cleaning, and searching for things in an overstuffed space. There's the opportunity cost of the physical space itself: rooms being used as storage that could be used for living.

Most people have never actually added these costs up. When you do, the math is sobering. The storage unit at $150 a month is $1,800 a year to house things you don't use and probably wouldn't miss. The extra bedroom that's become a dumping ground instead of a guest room or workspace. The closet so full you can't find what you're looking for, costing you twenty minutes a day in search time.

Clutter is expensive. It's just expensive in ways that don't show up on a single bill.

Distinguishing Clutter from Collections

Before we go further, there's a distinction this chapter needs to make clearly, because the rest of the book depends on it.

Not everything you own is clutter. Some things you own genuinely matter, genuinely bring you joy, genuinely represent who you are right now rather than who you thought you'd be.

There's a real difference between a cluttered person and a collector. Collectors keep specific things because those things have genuine meaning to them. Clutter is everything else — the accumulation that happened without intention, the objects kept out of guilt or inertia or the vague feeling that getting rid of them would be wrong.

The goal of this book is not to turn you into a minimalist with an empty house and a philosophical commitment to owning as little as possible. The goal is to help you get clear on which things actually belong in your life and which things are just taking up space.

If you have a collection that genuinely matters to you — stamps, books, art, whatever it might be — keeping it is not hoarding. It's curating. The question is whether the collection is serving you, or whether it's grown past the point where you can actually enjoy it and has started serving itself.

My own stamps are a good example. I had thousands. During a major purge I got rid of most of them — the ones I'd accumulated without much thought, the ones I kept because getting rid of them seemed like wasted money. But I kept the Tonga stamps and the Disney collection, because those are the ones I actually care about, the ones I look at and enjoy. What remained after the purge wasn't less of a collection. It was more of one — the actual collection, stripped of the accumulation that had buried it.

That distinction — between what you genuinely want and what you've simply not gotten around to dealing with — is the whole game. Once you can see it clearly, the decisions become much easier.

The Question That Changes Everything

Here's the question that cuts through all of the psychology described in this chapter:

Does this object serve your life as it actually is right now?

Not as it was. Not as you hope it will be. Not as you think it should be. As it actually is, today.

A kitchen gadget you bought for the cook you intended to become doesn't serve your actual life. A box of clothes that fit you ten years ago doesn't serve your actual life. A collection of books on subjects you no longer find interesting doesn't serve your actual life. An expensive hobby setup for a hobby you abandoned two years ago doesn't serve your actual life.

But a set of tools you use regularly serves your actual life. A collection you genuinely enjoy and return to serves your actual life. Books you actually read and reread serve your actual life.

The psychology described in this chapter — the survival instinct, the identity trap, the normalization problem, the emotional regulation mechanism — all of it is designed to keep you from asking this question clearly. Your brain has evolved to say "keep it" by default. The work of decluttering is overriding that default with honest assessment.

That's what the rest of this book will teach you to do.

If decluttering were a video game, choosing your method would be like picking your character class. Do you want to be the methodical wizard who organizes everything into perfect categories? The berserker who throws everything into boxes and sorts it out later? Or the ninja who sneaks around getting rid of one item at a time until nobody notices half the house is gone?

I've tried them all, mostly because I'm easily distracted by shiny new organizational theories. Let me save you some time and tell you what works and what sounds good on Instagram but will leave you crying in a pile of your own possessions.

Pinterest Method

The first method I encountered was what I call the Pinterest Method, though most people know it as the KonMari approach. Marie Kondo's book promised that if I just touched each item and asked myself whether it "sparked joy," I'd magically know what to keep and what to toss. Hold every single thing you own, feel its energy, and trust your intuition.

I decided to start with my book collection, which seemed reasonable since books were clearly defined objects with obvious purposes. I pulled the first book off the shelf, held it in my hands, and waited for the spark of joy.

Nothing.

I tried concentrating harder. I closed my eyes and really focused on the book. Still nothing. I started to wonder if maybe I was emotionally defective. Was I supposed to feel a literal spark? A warm glow? A sudden urge to hug the book?

After about ten minutes of trying to commune with a paperback copy of some thriller I'd read five years ago, I realized the fundamental flaw in this approach: most of my stuff had never sparked joy in the first place. I'd bought half of it because it was on sale, inherited a quarter of it from relatives, and accumulated the rest through the mysterious process by which households generate random objects like dust bunnies.

Asking whether something sparks joy assumes you had a passionate relationship with your possessions to begin with. Most of us have a relationship with our stuff that's more like a bad marriage: we've been together so long we've stopped noticing each other, and half the time we can't remember why we got together in the first place.

The KonMari method works great if you're the type of person who has deep emotional connections to your belongings and just needs permission to let go of the ones that don't serve you anymore. But if most of your stuff falls into the category of "I guess I need this?" or "someone gave this to me," you'll spend more time trying to manufacture feelings about objects than getting rid of them.

Minimalist Nuclear Option

After the KonMari experiment left me with a pile of books I'd handled but couldn't decide about, I swung in the opposite direction and tried what I call the Minimalist Nuclear Option. The basic premise is simple: get rid of everything except the absolute essentials. If you can live without it, it goes. If you haven't used it in six months, it goes. If you have to think about whether you need it, it goes.

I lasted exactly three days.

Extreme minimalism works great, if your goal is to live in a space that looks like a magazine but feels like a waiting room. I got rid of so much stuff that my apartment started to echo. I'd walk into my living room and feel like I should be holding a number and waiting for someone to call me up to a window.

More importantly, I realized I'd confused being minimalist with being miserable. Yes, I could survive with one plate, one cup, and one set of silverware. But washing dishes after every single meal wasn't making my life more peaceful. It was making me want to eat takeout off paper plates, which defeats the entire point of mindful living.

The minimalist approach assumes that less stuff automatically equals more happiness, but there's a sweet spot between drowning in possessions and living like a monk who's taken a vow of household poverty. Most of us need to find that middle ground where we have enough stuff to live comfortably but not so much that we spend all our time managing it.

Family Member Death Method

After the minimalist experiment left me sitting on the floor because I'd donated my couch as "unnecessary," I discovered what I call the Family Member Death Method. This one came naturally when relatives died and I had to think about what their accumulation meant — and what mine would mean to whoever had to deal with it someday.

Nothing gives you perspective on your own stuff like going through someone else's. When Claudia died, I spent the better part of a year pitching her belongings into garbage bins. Not donating, not selling — pitching. Looking at her things made me sad and angry, and the only way I could handle it was to get them out of my sight. Several huge bins' worth over twelve months. It was therapy disguised as housework.

Somewhere in that year I read a book called Not for Packrats Only, and it hit me at exactly the right moment. I was surrounded by evidence of what happens when someone dies and leaves their stuff behind. Claudia hadn't been a hoarder, but she'd had her things, and now those things were my problem to grieve and dispose of. The book made me look at my own accumulation with different eyes. Instead of seeing my belongings as extensions of my identity, I started seeing them as future problems for whoever had to clean up after me.

The death method is brutally effective because it strips away all the emotional nonsense we attach to our possessions. Dead people don't need their stuff. Dead people don't care if you donate their collection to charity or sell it on eBay. Dead people have moved on, literally and figuratively.

The death method works because it forces you to confront the reality that stuff is temporary but the burden of managing it gets passed on. It's like reverse estate planning: instead of thinking about what you want to leave to your family, you think about what you don't want to inflict on them.

But the death method has a major drawback: it's incredibly depressing. Spending too much time thinking about your own mortality and the ultimate meaninglessness of your possessions can send you into an existential spiral that makes you want to get rid of everything, including yourself.

Moving Day Panic Method

After a few weeks of the death method, I was ready to donate my entire life and move into a monastery. Then I stumbled onto what I now call the Moving Day Panic Method, which happened when my lease was up and I had exactly two weeks to pack everything I owned.

Nothing clarifies your relationship with your possessions like having to pick them up and put them in boxes. Suddenly, every item has to justify not just its existence in your life, but its worthiness to be wrapped in newspaper and transported to a new location.

The book you've been meaning to read for three years? Not worth the cardboard space. The decorative bowl that doesn't match anything else you own? Donation pile. The exercise equipment you bought during your short-lived fitness phase? Too heavy to move and too embarrassing to keep.

The moving method is brilliant because it adds a practical element to every decision. It's not just about whether you like something or whether it sparks joy. It's about whether you like it enough to spend time and energy moving it to your next home.

The downside of the moving method is that it's artificially stressful. Unless you're moving, you have to pretend you're under time pressure, which is exhausting. Plus, it tends to make you get rid of things that are genuinely useful just because they're heavy or awkward to pack.

The Fire Drill Method

Finally, I tried what I call the Fire Drill Method, which involves asking yourself one simple question about every item you own: "If the house was on fire and I could only save a few things, would this make the list?"

This method is wonderfully clarifying because it cuts through all the emotional attachment and practical justification to focus on what you'd grab if you had to run out the door. The fire drill method reveals the difference between what you think you value and what you value.

I discovered that in a real emergency, I wouldn't save my expensive art supplies or my carefully curated book collection. I'd grab my computer, some photos, maybe a change of clothes, and that would be it. Everything else, no matter how much I'd paid for it or how much I thought it meant to me, was replaceable.

The fire drill method is effective for sentimental items because it forces you to rank your emotional attachments. Yes, you love all twenty-seven coffee mugs your grandmother gave you over the years, but if you could only save three of them from a fire, which three would you choose? Keep those three, donate the rest.

But like all the other methods, the fire drill has limitations. It's great for identifying what's truly important to you, but it can be too extreme for everyday decluttering. Most of your possessions fall into a middle category where they're not important enough to save from a fire but are useful enough to keep around for normal life.

The Emotional Audit

Years later I developed what I now call the Emotional Audit. It goes considerably deeper than any of the other methods and addresses something the KonMari method doesn't reach at all: the emotional residue attached to objects from harmful relationships, difficult periods, and accumulated pain.

The method is straightforward, and it applies to physical and digital objects equally. Pick up each physical object — or open each digital folder, file, photo, or email thread — and ask yourself the eleven questions. Digital means everything: your computer, your phone, your tablet, cloud storage, backup drives, and anywhere else you've stored files and forgotten about them. The psychology is identical whether you're holding a box of old letters or scrolling through a folder of old photos on a cloud backup you haven't opened in four years. Digital storage is cheap, which means digital accumulation faces none of the natural pressure that physical clutter does. Nobody trips over a folder. Nobody runs out of drawer space because of old emails. The audit is the pressure that cheap storage removes.

The questions fall into three groups. The first is about memory and origin: Do I remember why I got this? Do I have good memories attached to it, or harmful ones? Was it an impulse acquisition? The second is about harm: Is it connected to someone or somewhere that harmed me? Am I keeping it because of obligation to another person rather than genuine want? How do I feel about it right now — not how I used to feel, right now? The third group are practical overrides that trump everything else: Does this still have real value in my current life? Is it legal where I live? Would it cause harm to someone I'm in a relationship with if they found it?

The operating principle: if the harmful memories outweigh the good, or if the object is connected to a relationship or period that did you damage, it goes. Mixed memories aren't automatically disqualifying — you're allowed to have complicated feelings about complicated things. But if holding the object produces more weight than warmth, that's your answer. An impulse buy with no emotional root at all? Also goes — inertia isn't a reason to keep something.

One caution: strong emotion doesn't automatically mean an object should go. Know what your tears signal before you start — for some people they mean harm, for others they mean love. Don't make permanent decisions in the middle of a wave of feeling.

There's a question you can add to the audit when the other eleven haven't given you a clear answer: is keeping this making my life better or smaller?

Not in the abstract. Concretely: does owning this object give you time, freedom, pleasure, capability? Or does it consume time, create obligation, generate guilt, and occupy space that could hold something you actually care about?

Objects that make your life better belong in it. Objects that make it smaller — that require maintenance without providing enjoyment, that represent who you meant to be rather than who you are, that stay because letting go is harder than keeping — those are the ones costing you something every day they remain.

The concept behind this book's title applies here: you're alive, and you have choices about how to spend that. Owning things that diminish your life is a choice you can unmake.

Two Final Questions That Override Everything Else

The illegal question catches things that wouldn't necessarily surface in an emotional audit. Laws vary by jurisdiction, and something legal where you bought it may not be legal where you live now. An unregistered firearm inherited from a relative. Prescription medication that isn't yours. A weapon that's legal in one state but not another. Items connected to past legal problems you'd rather not have rediscovered. These aren't always emergency-purge items, but asking the question directly — is this legal where I live right now — tends to produce a clear answer that inertia would otherwise let you avoid indefinitely.

The relationship question is the one I wish I'd known to ask earlier in my life. When I was married to Claudia, I had photographs of a previous girlfriend. Not hidden, not displayed — just there, in a box, through sheer inertia. I hadn't thought about them. I wasn't keeping them for any conscious reason. I simply hadn't asked the question.

Claudia found them. The previous girlfriend had been blonde. Claudia had jet black hair. What followed wasn't an argument that resolved and ended. It was a seed planted in the marriage that grew for twelve years. Would I be happier with a blonde?

Did I still have feelings for her? Was Claudia always going to be second choice? She never fully stopped wondering. That doubt, that low-level insecurity about whether she was enough, stayed in the marriage until the end.

The photographs had no emotional weight for me. They were just old paper in a box. But they carried enormous weight for her, and they carried it for twelve years because I never thought to ask: will keeping this cause harm to someone I love?

One question. One declutter session at any point in the years before she found them. Twelve years of doubt prevented. That's the cost of not asking it. The relationship question isn't about jealousy or controlling what you're allowed to keep. It's about being honest with yourself about what's actually in your home and what it might mean to someone who shares your life.

This applies everywhere you store things digitally — your phone, your computer, cloud storage, backup drives, old devices sitting in a drawer. A photo that would make you uncomfortable if found on your phone deserves the same question as one sitting in a physical box. An illegal file on a hard drive or a cloud backup carries the same risk as an illegal object in a drawer. The fact that it's on a device nobody looks at doesn't make it gone. Cheap storage makes it easy to never decide. The audit makes you decide anyway.

Where to start is a personal decision. My instinct is to go from worst to best — tackle the most emotionally charged objects first, the ones connected to trauma or harmful relationships, and work down to the ordinary room-by-room evaluation afterward. Most people find it easier to start with the obviously painless objects and work up toward the harder material gradually. Neither is wrong. But if you don't know where to begin at all, start with the easiest possible object in your entire home.

That object is in your junk drawer. It's probably even labeled junk. Start there. The drawer tells you what it is. Your only job is to agree with it. Clearing a junk drawer takes twenty minutes, costs you nothing emotionally, and gives you the first clear evidence that this process works. Build from that.

One button. That's the smallest unit of this process I've personally experienced. A single button from a piece of clothing that had belonged to my wife. Grief doesn't move in a straight line. After she died I cycled through love, anger, grief, and back again — sometimes all of it in the same afternoon. The button was carrying all of that. I threw it out. I felt better for a week. That's not a story about a button. It's a story about what the button was carrying. And about how much lighter you can feel when you stop carrying it.

The Emotional Audit is the method you use when the other methods don't get to the root of it. If you're standing in front of something and you can't let go despite having every logical reason to, the obstacle isn't practical. It's emotional. That's where this one starts.

The most important skill in the Four Piles system isn't organization. It's decision-making velocity.

Most people slow down because they're trying to make perfect decisions. They pick something up, consider it from every angle, put it back down, pick it up again. The session grinds to a halt. An hour passes and they've gotten through a third of a shelf.

The fix isn't to be less careful. It's to recognize that most decisions aren't as consequential as they feel in the moment. If you incorrectly donate something and later wish you had it, the consequence is usually minor — you buy another one, you live without it, or you realize you didn't actually need it after all. The catastrophic outcome of decluttering regret that your brain keeps warning you about almost never materializes.

Trust your first instinct. Pick something up, feel your gut response, assign it to a pile. If your gut says keep, keep it. If your gut says donate, donate it. Only stop to deliberate when the pull in both directions is genuinely equal — and even then, give yourself a strict time limit before it goes in the Decide Later pile.

The deciding-later pile has its own deadline, as described earlier. But it also has a size limit. If more than fifteen percent of what you're sorting ends up in Decide Later, you're using it as a way to avoid making decisions rather than as a genuine buffer.

The pile should be small and temporary, not a second storage location.

Conclusions

After trying all these approaches, I realized that no single method works for everyone or even for every situation. The key is understanding what each method is good for and using the right tool for the right job.

The KonMari method works great for people who have strong emotional connections to their belongings and need help sorting through those feelings. The minimalist approach is perfect for people who've already identified that they have too much stuff and want to be systematic about paring down. The death method is excellent for getting perspective on what's important. The moving method adds practical constraints that cut through indecision. The fire drill method helps you identify your real priorities.

The trick is to use different methods for different categories of stuff. Use the fire drill method for sentimental items to figure out what you care about. Use the moving method for practical items to determine what's worth the hassle of owning. Use the death method when you're feeling too attached to things that don't serve any real purpose in your life.

Use the Emotional Audit when none of the other methods are giving you a clear answer, or when you know the real obstacle isn't practical — it's emotional. If you're standing in front of something and you can feel resistance that has nothing to do with usefulness or value, run it through the eleven questions. The answer is almost always in there.

And when all else fails, use what I call the "Would I buy this today?" method. Look at something you already own and ask yourself honestly: if you were in a store right now and saw this exact item at the price you originally paid for it, would you buy it again?

Most of the time, the answer is no. You've changed, your tastes have evolved, your needs are different, or you've realized the thing wasn't as useful as you thought it would be. That's perfectly normal. You're allowed to change your mind about purchases you made in the past.

The goal isn't to find the perfect decluttering method. The goal is to get comfortable with making decisions about your stuff and to realize that most of those decisions aren't as important as they feel in the moment. Whether you keep something or get rid of it, the world isn't going to end.

Chapter 3: The Four Piles of Destiny

Once you've chosen your decluttering method, you need somewhere to put all the stuff you're making decisions about. This is where most people screw up. They start pulling things out of closets and drawers without any system for sorting them, and before they know it, their entire living room looks like a tornado hit a yard sale.

I learned this the hard way during my first serious decluttering attempt. I decided to tackle my bedroom closet, which seemed like a reasonable place to start since it was contained and I could close the door if things got ugly. I pulled everything out and dumped it on my bed, figuring I'd sort through it piece by piece.

Three hours later, I had a bed covered in clothes, shoes, boxes, and random objects I'd forgotten I owned. I'd made exactly zero decisions because every time I picked up an item, I'd find three more things underneath it that also needed attention. It was like playing the world's most frustrating game of Jenga, except instead of trying not to knock down blocks, I was trying not to have a nervous breakdown.

I realized I needed a system. Not some complicated organizational theory requiring color-coded labels and matching containers, but a simple way to sort things into categories that meant something.

Enter the Four Piles of Destiny. Well, technically they're five piles, but the fifth one is supposed to be temporary, though it has a way of becoming permanent if you're not careful.

Before you set up the four piles, there are a few practical decisions worth making.

Where will the piles live? Ideally in a space you can close off — a bedroom, a basement area — so you're not navigating around them when you're not actively sorting. The piles will be there for days or weeks. Don't put them somewhere that turns the decluttering project into a daily obstacle.

How will you handle items that need to leave immediately versus items that need to stay until you can deal with them? The trash pile should go to the actual trash same-day — don't let it sit. The donate pile can accumulate for a session or two before going to the car, but set a hard deadline: no donate pile survives more than two weeks without being transported. The sell pile needs its own space and a specific deadline — items not listed in thirty days move to donate.

Do you have help, or are you doing this alone? Both work. Doing it alone gives you the freedom to make decisions at your own pace without explaining yourself. Doing it with a trusted friend or partner can help with the decisions that need an outside perspective, and can provide accountability when the process slows down. The wrong kind of help — someone who either challenges every decision or defers to everything you say — is worse than no help at all.

Keep

The first pile is Keep. This is for stuff you use, need, or genuinely enjoy having around. The key word here is "genuinely." Not "I might enjoy this someday" or "I used to enjoy this" or "other people seem to enjoy this." If you can't remember the last time you used something or if picking it up doesn't make you feel at least neutral about owning it, it doesn't belong in the Keep pile.

I had to learn to be honest about the Keep pile because my natural instinct was to keep everything "just in case." I'd pick up a shirt I hadn't worn in two years and think, "But what if I need a shirt exactly this color for some specific occasion that might happen someday?" The answer, I learned, is that if such an occasion ever arises, I can buy a new shirt. The world has not run out of shirts.

The Keep pile should be one of the smaller piles when you're done. If it's the biggest pile, you're not really decluttering. You're just reorganizing your clutter, like rearranging deck chairs on the Titanic. It might look neater for a while, but you're still going down.

A few practical rules that help with the Keep pile:

If you haven't used something in a year, the burden of proof for keeping it should be high. "I might need it" isn't enough. "I will specifically need it for this identifiable purpose within the next three months" is more like it.

Duplicates are almost never justifiable. If you have three can openers and only one hand, you have two extra can openers. Keep the best one. The reasoning that you might need a backup if the main one breaks applies to almost nothing in a normal household. The hardware store exists for that scenario.

Sentimental value is real, but it has limits. An object can carry genuine meaning without earning permanent space in your home. The question isn't whether something meant something to you once. It's whether it's earning its keep in your life right now.

The Keep pile has a natural enemy: the feeling that you're being wasteful by getting rid of things. You paid for this. You might need it. Someone could use it. These are all thoughts designed to move things from the other piles back into Keep. Recognize them for what they are and apply them strictly only to things you actually use.

Sell

The second pile is Sell. This is for stuff that's in good condition and worth enough money to justify the hassle of selling it. The key phrase here is "justify the hassle." Selling things takes time and energy. You must take photos, write descriptions, deal with potential buyers, handle shipping or meetups, and manage the entire transaction.

For most items, the amount of money you'll get isn't worth the time and aggravation involved. That decorative bowl you paid thirty dollars for five years ago? You might get five dollars for it on eBay, if you're lucky. After you factor in the time spent listing it, the fees, and the cost of shipping materials, you're working for less than minimum wage.

I made this mistake early in my decluttering work. I spent weeks trying to sell things on eBay that I should have just donated. I'd take photos, research prices, write detailed descriptions, and then watch the items sit unsold for days. When they finally did sell, I'd make three or four dollars after fees. I was spending hours of my life to earn less money than I could make in ten minutes at my regular job.

The Sell pile should be reserved for items that are either genuinely valuable or hold their value well. Electronics that are less than a few years old, designer clothing in good condition, collectibles that people search for, tools that cost more than fifty dollars when new. If something is worth less than twenty dollars and you're not emotionally attached to getting money for it, skip the Sell pile and move it directly to Donate.

A realistic sell threshold: if the item would sell for less than twenty dollars and requires more than fifteen minutes of your time to photograph, list, and ship, donate it instead. Your time has value. Spending an hour to make eight dollars after fees isn't decluttering — it's a very inefficient part-time job.

The exceptions are items worth real money: electronics less than three years old, brand-name clothing in excellent condition, collectibles with an identifiable market, tools and equipment that cost over a hundred dollars when new. These are worth the effort. A bread maker you bought for fifty dollars in 2015 is not.

eBay and Facebook Marketplace serve different categories. eBay is better for collectibles, vintage items, and things with a national buyer pool. Facebook Marketplace is better for furniture, large items, and things someone local would want to pick up in person. Craigslist still works for furniture and large items in many markets. Know which platform fits what you're selling before you start.

One practical tip: photograph everything in the Sell pile on the same day before anything gets moved. Once items start migrating or getting mixed up, you'll waste time re-photographing and re-identifying things.

Donate

The third pile is Donate. This is where most of your discarded stuff should end up. Items that are in decent condition but not valuable enough to sell, clothes that don't fit but aren't worn out, books you'll never read again, kitchen gadgets that work but that you never use.

The beauty of the Donate pile is that it removes the guilt factor from getting rid of things. You're not throwing away perfectly good items. You're giving them to someone who might need or want them. That jacket you never wear might be exactly what someone at the thrift store is looking for. Those books gathering dust on your shelf might find their way to someone who'll love reading them.

The Donate pile also has a practical advantage: it's easy to get rid of. You can drop everything off at Goodwill or the Salvation Army in one trip. You don't have to take photos, write descriptions, or deal with buyers. You just dump everything off and drive away.

I learned to love the Donate pile because it made me feel good about decluttering instead of guilty. Instead of feeling like I was wasting money by getting rid of things I'd paid for, I felt like I was doing something positive by passing them on to people who would use them.

The Donate pile works best when you remove the friction from actually donating things. The single biggest reason donation piles don't get donated is that they sit in a corner or in the trunk of a car for months because the logistics never got resolved.

Before you start your decluttering session, identify your donation destination. Most cities have a Goodwill, Salvation Army, Habitat for Humanity ReStore, or similar organization. Many offer pickup for larger items. Some have restrictions on what they accept — no broken electronics, no stained clothing, no incomplete sets. Knowing this before you sort prevents the pile from getting stuck.

A donation bag that lives in your closet on an ongoing basis — separate from the active decluttering pile — is useful for the steady trickle of things you decide to let go throughout the year. When you try on something that doesn't fit and never will, it goes in the bag rather than back on the hanger. When the bag is full, it goes to the car. When it's in the car, it gets dropped off within a week.

Trash

The fourth pile is Trash. This is for stuff that's broken, worn out, stained, missing pieces, or otherwise not suitable for donation. Be honest about what belongs in this pile. That shirt with the hole in the armpit that you keep thinking you'll mend someday? Trash. The electronics that stopped working two years ago but that you've kept because "maybe they can be fixed"? Trash. The puzzle that's missing half the pieces? Trash.

Americans have a weird relationship with throwing things away. We feel guilty about putting things in the trash, even when they're genuinely worthless. We've been trained to think that everything can be repaired, repurposed, or recycled, noble in theory but impractical.

Some things are just trash. It's okay to throw them away. You're not a bad person for admitting that something has reached the end of its useful life. In fact, you're being more honest than the person who donates broken items and makes them someone else's problem.

The Trash pile serves an important psychological function too. It forces you to confront the reality that some of your purchases were mistakes. That exercise equipment that broke the first time you used it? That was a bad purchase, and keeping it around isn't going to change that fact. Throwing it away is like admitting the mistake and moving on.

Americans donate too much and trash too little. This sounds backwards, but it's true.

Donating broken, stained, worn-out, or incomplete items isn't generosity — it's making your problem someone else's problem.

Goodwill doesn't want your broken blender. The Salvation Army doesn't need your shirt with the armpit stain. Donating unusable items wastes the time of the people who have to sort and discard them at the receiving end.

If something is broken and can't be easily fixed, trash it. If something is stained or worn past the point of being wearable, trash it. If something is missing pieces and is therefore functionless, trash it. This is not waste. This is honest.

The resistance to trashing things comes from the same place as the resistance to letting go in general — a feeling that the money you spent on something is preserved in the object, and throwing the object away means losing the money. The money is already gone. The question is whether you want the broken thing to come with it.

I'll Decide Later

A friend of mine named Priya had a pile in her living room that had been there for eight months. Not a small pile — a serious presence, about four feet wide and two feet high, sitting against the wall like it had always been there. She'd walk past it every day, sometimes moving things off the top and onto the pile when they didn't have anywhere else to go.

She told me she needed to "go through it properly when she had a free day." Eight months passed. No free day appeared.

When I came over and we looked at it together, the paralysis became clear immediately. Every item had at least one reason she wasn't sure about. The box of photos she should really sort and organize. The old paperwork that might be important but probably wasn't. The gifts from relatives she didn't know what to do with. The things that belonged to rooms she hadn't decided about yet.

None of these were hard decisions individually. They were just decisions she hadn't made.

I told her the rule: pick it up once, put it somewhere that isn't the pile. Keep, donate, trash — one touch, one destination, no returns to the pile. If you can't decide, trash bag, two-week deadline.

She pushed back. She wanted to go through the photos properly. She wanted to check what the paperwork was before discarding it. I said fine — sort the photos in one session, check the paperwork in one session. But every item gets a next destination today.

Three hours. The pile was gone.

She called the next day and said it felt like the room was bigger. It wasn't. But it felt that way because the open loop was closed.

Now, about that fifth pile I mentioned. This is the "I'll Decide Later" pile, and it's both the most useful and most dangerous part of the whole system.

The "I'll Decide Later" pile exists because some decisions are genuinely difficult and you don't want to get stuck on them during your initial sorting. You're going through a drawer and you find something you're not sure about. Maybe it's sentimental but you're not sure how sentimental. Maybe it's useful but you're not sure how useful. Instead of stopping your momentum to debate with yourself for twenty minutes, you put it in the "I'll Decide Later" pile and keep moving.

The danger is that if you're not careful, the "I'll Decide Later" pile becomes a permanent storage solution. You finish sorting everything else, but the difficult items just sit there in their pile, taking up space and mocking your indecision.

I learned to manage the "I'll Decide Later" pile by giving it a deadline. Everything in that pile had to be decided within a week. If I couldn't make a decision about something in a week, it went straight to Donate. The reasoning was that if I couldn't decide whether I wanted something after thinking about it for a week, I probably didn't want it very much.

This deadline approach worked because it forced me to realize that most of the items in the "I'll Decide Later" pile weren't really that important to me. I was just having trouble letting go of them because I'd owned them for a long time or because I'd paid money for them. But neither of those is a good reason to keep something.

Conclusions

The most common mistake people make with the Four Piles system is treating the Sell pile as a place where value is preserved rather than a place where value is converted.

The point of the Sell pile isn't to get back what you paid. That's not happening. The point is to convert things that are taking up space into cash that you can actually use — and to do so efficiently enough that the time cost doesn't exceed the financial return.

Set your threshold before you start: anything worth less than X dollars goes directly to donate, regardless of what you paid for it. Twenty dollars is a reasonable floor for most people. If you're comfortable with eBay and have time to manage listings, you might lower it to ten. If time is tight, raise it to fifty.

The second common mistake is allowing the Decide Later pile to expand indefinitely. The pile is a buffer for genuine uncertainty, not a way to avoid making decisions. If more than one in ten items is going into Decide Later, you're using it as an escape hatch. Set the deadline before you start: everything in that pile gets decided within a week, or it goes to donate automatically.

The third common mistake is sorting without a destination plan. You fill the donate boxes, and they sit in your garage for three months because you never figured out where they were going. Make the phone call before the session, not after.

A note on the boring middle ground, because it's where most of the work actually happens.

The Emotional Audit in Chapter 2 is designed for objects with emotional weight — things connected to significant relationships, difficult periods, or genuine sentimental value. It's not designed for the seventy boxes of ordinary household stuff that has no dramatic emotional content either way. That stuff doesn't need eleven questions. It needs three.

Do I use it? Not "did I once use it" or "might I use it someday." Have I used it in the past year? If no, what changes in the next year that would make me use it? If you can't name a specific change, that's a no.

Does it work? Broken things waiting to be fixed, incomplete things missing pieces, things that "mostly" work — these have a way of living in Decide Later forever. Set a rule before you start: if it doesn't work and you haven't fixed it in six months, it goes. If it does work but you never use it, apply the first question.

Do I have too many? Most households have multiples of things they only need one of. Four can openers. Seventeen coffee mugs. Three sets of the same kitchen tools. Keep the best one. Donate the rest. No emotional archaeology required.

These three questions handle the vast majority of ordinary household clutter without requiring you to audit your feelings about every item you've ever owned. Save the eleven questions for the objects that genuinely have weight. The rest is just stuff, and stuff doesn't need that much of your attention.

The Four Piles of Destiny work because they force you to make decisions about your stuff instead of just moving it around. Every item has to go somewhere, and each destination means something different. Keep means you're committing to storing, maintaining, and making space for something. Sell means you're willing to invest time and energy to get money for something. Donate means you're ready to let go of something but want it to go to good use. Trash means you're admitting something has no value to anyone.

The piles also help you see patterns in your accumulation habits. If your Trash pile is huge, you might have a problem with buying cheap, low-quality items that don't last. If your Donate pile is full of clothes with tags still on them, you might have a shopping addiction or trouble understanding what you like. If your Sell pile is mostly expensive items you never used, you might be buying aspirational objects that don't match your lifestyle.

I discovered that my Donate pile was always full of books. Not just any books, but specific types of books I bought because I thought I should read them, not because I wanted to read them. Business books that were supposed to make me more successful. Self-help books that were supposed to make me a better person. Classic novels that were supposed to make me more cultured.

All these books sat on my shelves making me feel guilty because I'd bought them with good intentions but never read them. Getting rid of them was like admitting that I wasn't the person I'd thought I wanted to be when I bought them. But keeping them wasn't making me into that person either. It was just making me feel bad about not being that person.

The Four Piles of Destiny aren't magic. They won't make difficult decisions easier, and they won't change your emotional relationship with your possessions. But they will give you a framework for making progress instead of just moving stuff around.

The key is to trust the system and stick with your decisions. Don't second-guess yourself. Don't rescue things from the Donate pile because you suddenly remember how much you paid for them. Don't let the "I'll Decide Later" pile become a permanent storage solution.

Your stuff wants to be useful. If it's not useful to you, let it go be useful to someone else. The world doesn't need more storage units full of things that nobody's using. It needs people who are comfortable making decisions about what belongs in their lives and what doesn't.

After a few decluttering sessions, you'll start to notice your own patterns in the piles.

If your Trash pile is unusually large, you've been holding onto broken, worn-out, and unusable things because letting go felt wasteful. The practical lesson: buy better-quality items less often, and don't keep things past their useful life out of guilt.

If your Donate pile is full of things with tags still on them or items in original packaging, you have an impulse buying pattern. You're acquiring things faster than you can integrate them into your life. The practical lesson: add a waiting period to significant purchases. If you still want it in two weeks, buy it. Most impulse purchases don't survive two weeks of reconsideration.

If your Sell pile is mostly expensive items you never used, you have a pattern of aspirational purchasing — buying equipment for the person you intend to become rather than the person you are. The practical lesson: borrow or rent before you buy anything related to a new interest. If the interest persists through three rental experiences, then you own the equipment.

If the Keep pile keeps wanting to be bigger than the others, you haven't yet made the psychological shift from "why would I get rid of this?" to "why does this deserve space in my life?" That shift is the whole work of this book. The piles just reveal where you are in making it.

When the four-pile system isn't giving you a clear answer and something has been in the Decide Later pile for a week with no resolution, ask this: is keeping this making my life better?

Not potentially better. Not theoretically better. Right now, in your actual daily life — does owning this object give you anything? Does it give you joy, utility, capability, pleasure? Or does it give you guilt, obligation, clutter, and one more thing to work around?

If you can't articulate a specific way it's improving your current life, it's making your life smaller by occupying space that something better could occupy. That's enough reason to let it go.

The Four Piles of Destiny teach you how to make decisions about your stuff and live with the consequences. It's a skill that gets easier with practice, and once you learn it, you'll never go back to just moving your clutter around.

Chapter 4: The Emergency Purge: Get Rid of This Stuff FIRST

Before we get into the philosophical aspects of decluttering and the emotional process of letting go, there's some stuff you need to get rid of right now. Not tomorrow, not after you finish reading this book, not when you get around to it. Today.

I'm talking about the items in your house that could literally ruin your life if the wrong person found them at the wrong time. The stuff that could end your marriage, cost you your job, get you arrested, or cause you serious embarrassment if you died tomorrow and someone else had to go through your belongings.

You know what I'm talking about. We all have things we'd rather nobody else ever saw. The difference between smart people and people who get featured in cautionary tales is that smart people get rid of the dangerous stuff before it becomes a problem.

Let me tell you about my friend Mike, who learned this lesson the hard way. Mike was going through a messy divorce, and his soon-to-be-ex-wife had hired an aggressive lawyer. During the discovery phase, they subpoenaed everything: financial records, computer files, phone records, the works.

Mike thought he was prepared. He'd hired his own lawyer, organized his important documents, and figured he had nothing to hide. Then the lawyer asked him about the storage unit he'd been renting for three years.

Mike had completely forgotten about the storage unit. He'd rented it during a previous move and just kept paying the monthly fee without thinking about what was in there. Turns out, it was full of stuff from his bachelor days: magazines that wouldn't look good in family court, party photos that suggested a lifestyle incompatible with custody arguments, and financial records from some questionable business ventures.

None of it was illegal, but all of it painted a picture Mike didn't want his lawyer to have to explain to a judge. By the time he remembered the storage unit existed, it was too late to clean it out without looking like he was hiding evidence.

Mike's divorce cost him an extra fifty thousand dollars in legal fees and a less favorable custody arrangement, all because he'd forgotten about a storage unit full of stuff that should have been thrown away years earlier.

Don't be Mike.

The items I'm about to describe fall into different categories of danger, but they all have one thing in common: the longer you keep them, the more likely they are to cause you serious problems.

Anything Illegal

First up: anything illegal. I don't care how minor it seems or how long you've had it. That prescription medication from your back surgery five years ago? It's illegal to possess expired controlled substances. Those fireworks you bought in another state? They might be illegal in your state. That software you downloaded that you're pretty sure isn't properly licensed? It's stealing.

The "I forgot I had this" defense doesn't work in court. Neither does "I was going to get rid of it eventually" or "everyone does this." If it's illegal to possess, get rid of it today.

My friend Jeff learned this lesson from his own stupidity. After Jeff's dad died, he was going through his father's belongings and found a small handgun in a shoebox. Jeff's dad had bought it legally years earlier, but he'd never bothered to register it when he moved to a state with different gun laws. For three years after his father's death, Jeff had an unregistered firearm sitting in his closet because he didn't want to deal with the paperwork of disposing of it properly.

Three years. An unregistered gun in Jeff's house for three years because he was too lazy to make a phone call to the police about proper disposal. If anyone had searched Jeff's house for any reason during that time, he would have been arrested for illegal weapons possession. All because he didn't want to spend an afternoon dealing with something that should have been handled immediately.

The practical steps for common illegal items: prescription medications that aren't yours or have expired can be taken to most pharmacy drop-off programs — the DEA runs regular take-back events, and many pharmacies accept them year-round. This is free and anonymous. Firearms should be taken to your local police station for disposal or transferred to a licensed dealer if they have value. Unlicensed software should simply be deleted and the programs uninstalled. Expired fireworks should be soaked in water and discarded — do not attempt to dispose of them dry.

The key is not to let the logistics of proper disposal become an excuse for indefinite delay. One phone call, one trip, one afternoon solves most of these situations. The longer you wait, the higher the risk grows.

Relationship Landmines

The relationship landmine problem deserves more attention than it usually gets, because it operates in both directions.

The first direction is obvious: things you own that would hurt your partner if discovered. The photographs, the correspondence, the evidence of connections you've maintained without being forthcoming about them. The second direction is less obvious: things you own that represent a version of yourself your partner has never seen or doesn't know about, and that would require explanation you're not prepared to give.

This second category isn't necessarily shameful. It might be an old hobby your partner doesn't know you had. A period of your life you haven't fully shared. Correspondence from people who mattered to you before your current relationship in ways that are complicated to explain.

The question isn't whether you have anything to hide in a moral sense. The question is whether the things you're keeping would hurt your partner to discover, require a conversation you haven't had, or quietly damage something you care about. If the answer is yes, the appropriate response isn't necessarily to get rid of everything — in some cases it's to have the conversation. But you can't have the conversation about things you've forgotten you own. The audit surfaces them so you can make a choice.

Recovery from Addiction

The recovery category deserves particular care because the stakes are higher than any other item in this chapter.

Addiction recovery is fragile in ways that are hard to fully convey to someone who hasn't experienced it. The brain's relationship to the substance or behavior it became dependent on doesn't simply reset when the active use stops. Triggers — sensory cues associated with the addictive behavior — can activate craving at full intensity years into recovery, seemingly without warning. An object associated with the substance doesn't need to be used to be a problem. Its presence in the environment is itself a trigger.

This means the question isn't whether you're strong enough to have that bottle in the house. It's whether there's any benefit to the risk. There isn't. The bottle doesn't provide anything. The memories it might hold are accessible without it. The cost of it being there — the cognitive tax of knowing it's there, the accumulated small exposures to a trigger — is entirely unnecessary.

The same logic applies to anything associated with the addictive behavior: paraphernalia, memorabilia, photographs from periods of active use that are more trigger than memory. The goal isn't to erase your history. It's to stop maintaining a physical environment that makes the most dangerous parts of your history more accessible than they need to be.

If you're in recovery and you have these items, get rid of them. Not eventually. Now. The logistics of disposal are simpler than they feel — most of this category is trash, donation, or a five-minute conversation with your sponsor about what to do with the rest.

Professional Suicide Items

The professional suicide category deserves more attention than it usually gets, because the digital component has expanded dramatically.

It's no longer just about physical items — a company laptop in a closet, confidential documents in a filing cabinet. Your work life leaves a digital trail that can create problems long after the specific situation is resolved.

Work emails sent from a personal account. Documents saved to personal cloud storage when you were working remotely. Screenshots of internal communications. Conversations in messaging apps that included confidential client or company information. These exist in the same device you're using right now, often forgotten, occasionally a serious problem if discovered during a legal dispute, an HR investigation, or a divorce proceeding where financial discovery is involved.

The practical step: when you leave any job, spend an afternoon cleaning out the professional residue. Delete work-related files from personal devices. Remove work email accounts from personal apps. Delete saved passwords for work systems. If you worked remotely and saved anything to personal cloud storage that should have stayed on work systems, delete it. This isn't about covering your tracks — it's about maintaining appropriate boundaries between your professional and personal digital life, which protects both you and your former employer.

For current employees: the same principle applies. Keeping work information on personal devices creates risk for you regardless of your intentions. If you need access to work files, use work systems. If something ends up on a personal device, deal with it before it becomes a problem.

Safety Hazards

Safety hazards are the items most people underestimate until something goes wrong. Anything that could hurt someone if it broke, leaked, exploded, or caught fire. Old paint cans in the garage that you're not sure what they contain. Cleaning chemicals that are so old the labels have worn off. Electronics that spark when you plug them in but that you keep because they "still work sometimes."

Safety hazards have a way of becoming emergencies at the worst possible times. That space heater that sometimes smells funny will wait until you have house guests to catch fire. Those mystery chemicals in the garage will wait until your curious neighbor's kid finds them to become a poison control emergency.

I had a friend whose garage burned down because he'd stored old paint cans next to a water heater. The fire department said the cans had been leaking fumes for months before they finally ignited. He lost his garage, his car, and nearly his house because he didn't want to pay the disposal fee for hazardous materials.

The disposal fee was twenty dollars. The fire damage was forty thousand.

A Special Note About Children and Pets: If you have kids or animals in your house, safety hazards become even more dangerous. Children are naturally curious and will find ways to get into things you thought were safely stored. That bottle of drain cleaner under the sink? A toddler will figure out how to open the childproof cap faster than you can. Those interesting-looking berries from the decorative plant you forgot was poisonous? Your dog will eat them.

I know a couple whose four-year-old managed to get into a locked toolbox and found some old batteries that had started leaking acid. The kid thought they were toys. One emergency room visit and several hundred dollars later, they learned that "childproof" doesn't mean "child-impossible," it just means "child-delayed."

If you have little ones around, be thorough about getting rid of anything that could hurt them. Kids don't read warning labels, and pets don't understand that the shiny liquid in the pretty bottle isn't water. What seems obviously dangerous to you might look like the most interesting thing in the world to a curious three-year-old or a bored cat.

The rule is simple: if you wouldn't want a child or pet to get their hands (or paws) on it, get it out of your house entirely. Don't just put it up high or lock it away. Kids are escape artists, and pets are surprisingly resourceful when they want to investigate something.

Hazardous material disposal is easier than most people assume, which makes the "I don't know what to do with it" excuse weaker than it appears.

Old paint: many hardware stores and municipal waste facilities accept latex paint for recycling. Oil-based paint requires hazardous waste disposal — call your city or county for the schedule. Paint that has dried solid in the can is no longer hazardous and can usually go in regular trash.

Batteries: most big-box stores have battery recycling bins near the entrance. This takes thirty seconds.

Electronics: e-waste facilities accept computers, phones, televisions, and most electronics. Many municipalities run periodic e-waste collection events. Best Buy accepts most consumer electronics for recycling at no charge.

Cleaning chemicals and unknown substances: your county hazardous waste facility handles these. Most run regular collection days. Call before you go to confirm they accept what you have.

The pattern is the same in every case: one phone call or one web search tells you where to go. The disposal takes one trip. The obstacle is almost never the logistics — it's deciding to deal with it.

Identity Theft Goldmines

Identity theft goldmines deserve their own attention, because the risk is less dramatic than fire or legal trouble but nearly as consequential. Old financial documents, expired credit cards, documents with your social security number, old driver's licenses, anything with personal information that you don't need anymore.

Identity thieves love people who keep old financial documents because it gives them everything they need to open accounts in your name. That bank statement from 2015 might not seem important to you, but it's treasure to someone who wants to steal your identity.

I used to keep every financial document I'd ever received because I thought I might need them for taxes or disputes. My filing cabinet was full of bank statements, credit card bills, and investment statements going back fifteen years. I felt very organized and responsible.

Then I realized I was keeping a complete roadmap of my financial life in a filing cabinet that anyone could break into. Every account number, every address I'd lived at, every piece of personal information someone would need to impersonate me financially.

Now I keep financial documents for two years, then shred everything. If I need something older than that, I can get it from the bank or credit card company. But I'm not keeping a burglary kit for identity thieves in my filing cabinet anymore.

The nuclear option for all of this is what I call the "death test." Look at every questionable item you own and ask yourself: "If I died tomorrow and my family had to go through my stuff, would I be embarrassed about them finding this?"

If the answer is yes, get rid of it. Your privacy dies with you, but your reputation lives on in the memories of the people who have to clean up after you.

Conclusions

Identity theft is the category most people think they understand until they actually go through their old documents and realize what's in there.

Financial documents aren't the only risk. Old medical records contain your full name, address, date of birth, insurance information, and sometimes Social Security numbers. Employment records contain similar information. Expired passports and driver's licenses contain everything an identity thief needs. Old tax returns are a comprehensive guide to your financial history.

The two-year retention rule covers most purposes: the IRS can audit returns going back three years in standard cases, so keeping your last three years of tax documents provides adequate protection. Everything older than that from a non-tax source can be shredded.

Shredding matters. A trash can full of torn bank statements is not adequate protection. Cross-cut shredders are inexpensive, take thirty seconds per document, and eliminate the risk entirely. If you have a large volume to destroy, most office supply stores offer shredding services by the pound.

The items most people overlook: old checkbooks, especially ones from closed accounts. Pre-approved credit card offers that arrived in the mail and were set aside. Utility bills from previous addresses. Medical explanation-of-benefits documents. Old cell phone contracts. All of these contain enough personal information to create problems in the wrong hands.

The emergency purge isn't about paranoia. It's about recognizing that certain things in your home are actively working against your ability to live well. Every item in this chapter sits in your life as a liability — something that can reduce your freedom, your relationships, your security, or your safety. Carrying liabilities isn't living. It's managing risk while your actual life waits.

Dead people have no secrets. Everything you own will be seen, handled, and judged by someone else eventually. The only question is whether you want to control what they find or leave it to chance.

The emergency purge isn't about being paranoid or assuming the worst about people. It's about taking control of your risk and not leaving potential disasters sitting around your house like unexploded bombs.

You've worked too hard to build your life to let it be destroyed by stuff you forgot you owned. Clean out the dangerous items now, while you can still control the narrative.

Your future self will thank you for eliminating the threats you can control.

The through-line of the emergency purge chapter is simple: the things most likely to cause you serious harm are almost never the things you consciously worry about. They're the things you've forgotten about, the things that accumulated without your attention, the things sitting in storage units or desk drawers or old hard drives that you haven't thought about in years.

The purpose of going through this list isn't to make you paranoid. It's to make you deliberate. Most people have never conducted a systematic review of what they own and what risks it carries. One afternoon spent doing this — really doing it, not just mentally noting that you should someday — eliminates a class of problems that could otherwise surface at the worst possible moments.

The phone call you don't want to receive. The discovery your lawyer wasn't expecting. The conversation you'd rather not have. These outcomes aren't inevitable, but they're far less likely after you've addressed the items in this chapter.

Do it once. Do it thoroughly. Then maintain it annually as part of the broader maintenance practice described later in this book.

Chapter 5: The 20 Sacred Excuses (And Why They're All Bullshit)

Now that you've gotten rid of the truly dangerous stuff, it's time to tackle the hardest part of decluttering: the lies you tell yourself about why you need to keep everything else.

I've heard every excuse in the book for keeping clutter, and I've used most of them myself. They sound so reasonable when you're standing there holding something you don't want to throw away. They're logical, practical, and emotionally satisfying. They're also complete nonsense.

These excuses are your brain's way of protecting you from the discomfort of making decisions and letting go of things. Your subconscious has figured out that if it can come up with a good enough reason to keep something, you'll stop questioning whether you need it.

The problem is that these excuses multiply like rabbits. Start accepting one, and suddenly everything in your house has a perfectly reasonable justification for staying exactly where it is. Before you know it, you're not decluttering at all. You're just moving stuff around while telling yourself stories about why each item is essential to your survival.

I've organized these excuses into families because they tend to travel in packs. Once you start using one type of excuse, you'll find yourself using all the variations. Learn to recognize the patterns, and you'll get better at catching yourself before you fall into the trap.

What makes the excuses in this chapter different from the ones you've probably seen catalogued in other decluttering books is this: every one of them is costing you something right now. Not someday when you die and someone has to sort through your things. Right now, today. The broken leaf blower taking up floor space in your garage is costing you the use of that floor space. The clothes that don't fit are costing you clarity every time you open the closet. The expensive gadget you feel guilty about is costing you a small amount of energy every time you see it.

The excuses feel like they're protecting you from the discomfort of letting go. What they're actually doing is keeping you in a continuous low-grade tax on your time, attention, and living space. Every excuse you accept is a vote for continuing to pay that tax.

There's something worth understanding about why the excuses keep working: humans are wired to avoid acute discomfort even when it means accepting chronic discomfort. The one-time cost of a decision — picking something up, feeling the resistance, choosing a pile — is acute. You feel it right now, immediately, in the moment. The ongoing cost of keeping something you don't need — the space it occupies, the energy it takes each time you see it, the guilt that doesn't quite go away — is chronic. You barely notice it because you're always paying it.

The excuses are your brain's way of protecting you from the acute cost by keeping you locked into the chronic one. Each individual excuse sounds reasonable. What it's actually doing is trading a one-time payment for a subscription you didn't consciously sign up for. The decision takes five minutes. The alternative runs indefinitely.

The "Someday" Family of Excuses

This is the most popular excuse family because it sounds so hopeful and forward-thinking. Who doesn't want to believe in a magical future where everything you've saved will suddenly become useful?

Excuse #1: "I might need it someday."

This is the mother of all decluttering excuses. My dad Jerry was the master of it. The garage filled up with equipment for every outdoor activity he might someday pursue. A raft we used once and never again. Gardening tools for a garden that stayed hypothetical for decades. Camping gear for trips that never happened. Each item bought for a future version of himself that never quite arrived.

The problem with "someday" is that it never arrives. Or when it does, you can't find the thing you saved, or you've forgotten you had it, or it's been sitting in a damp basement for so long that it's no longer functional.

Here's the reality check: if you haven't needed something in the past year, you probably won't need it in the next year. And if you do need it, you can probably buy or borrow a replacement for less money than you're spending to store the original.

Excuse #2: "What if they stop making these?"

My mom Valerie was convinced that manufacturers were constantly discontinuing perfectly good products just to spite her. She'd buy multiple bottles of shampoo when she found one she liked because "what if they stop making it?" She had backup supplies of everything: toothpaste, soap, makeup, cleaning products.

Valerie's bathroom looked like she was preparing for the apocalypse. She had enough personal care products to supply a small hotel. Most of them expired before she could use them, but she kept buying more because you never know when your favorite brand might disappear forever.

The truth is that if a product is good enough for you to want to hoard it, it's probably popular enough that the company won't stop making it. And if they do discontinue it, they'll replace it with something similar. The world is not going to run out of shampoo, and you don't need to personally maintain a strategic reserve.

Excuse #3: "I'll fix it when I have time."

This excuse is responsible for more garage clutter than any natural disaster. Broken lawn mowers that just need a new spark plug. Furniture with wobbly legs that just needs to be tightened. Electronics that work fine except for that one thing.

Jerry had the same logic with his outdoor gear and art supplies. The raft that just needed a new valve. The easel with the broken hinge he was going to repair. Canvases he'd started and set aside until he had the right brushes. The occasion or the inspiration rarely came. The equipment accumulated.

My parents never threw out a piece of broken equipment in their lives. They had a console entertainment unit — TV, record player, and 8-track all in one cabinet — that weighed over 200 pounds. When I was ten, I pulled apart two of their other broken tube TVs for parts and kept them in a box. When my father's apartment was cleaned out after he died, that box was still there, parts untouched. As for the console, as far as I know it was still sitting in their house when they abandoned it in their seventies. They moved out. The console stayed.

If you haven't fixed something within six months of it breaking, you're probably never going to fix it. Either fix it now or get rid of it. Don't let broken things take up space while you pretend you're going to get around to them eventually.

Excuse #4: "I might take up that hobby again."

This excuse is painful because it involves admitting that you've changed or that your past interests no longer excite you. Nobody wants to acknowledge that the person they used to be isn't the person they are now.

I held onto art supplies for years after I stopped drawing regularly. Expensive brushes, half-empty tubes of paint, canvases I'd bought with enthusiasm but never used. I kept telling myself I'd get back into art when I had more time, when I was less stressed, when I had better light in my apartment.

The art supplies sat in a corner, making me feel guilty every time I looked at them. They represented the creative person I thought I should be, not the person I was. Admitting that I wasn't going to take up drawing again was like admitting that part of my identity was gone.

But here's what I learned: letting go of the supplies didn't kill my ability to be creative. If I ever wanted to draw again, I could buy new supplies. Keeping the old ones wasn't preserving my creativity. It was just making me feel bad about not using them.

The "Money" Family of Excuses

These excuses are all about protecting yourself from the feeling that you've wasted money. They're insidious because they disguise themselves as being financially responsible.

Excuse #5: "It was expensive!"

This excuse assumes that the money you spent on something is somehow preserved in the object itself, and that getting rid of the object means losing the money. It's like thinking that if you don't eat the expensive meal you ordered but don't want, you'll get your money back.

Valerie had an exercise bike that she'd bought for six hundred dollars and used exactly three times. It sat in her bedroom for eight years, covered with clothes that needed to be hung up. She couldn't get rid of it because "it was expensive," even though it had become a very costly clothing rack.

The expensive items are often the hardest to let go of because they represent bigger financial mistakes. But keeping them doesn't undo the mistake. It just extends the consequences.

Excuse #6: "I paid good money for this!"

This is the angry version of "it was expensive." It's the excuse you use when you're frustrated about a purchase that didn't work out and you want someone or something to blame.

Jerry had a collection of tools and outdoor equipment that he'd accumulated over the years, convinced that having the right gear would make him better at whatever activity he was planning. He'd research the best brands, read reviews, and spend serious money on equipment he'd use once and then forget about.

The amount you paid for something has no relationship to its current value to you. A tool you paid two hundred dollars for but haven't used in five years is less valuable than a ten-dollar tool you use every week.

Excuse #7: "It might be worth something someday."

This excuse turns your house into a speculative investment portfolio where everything might suddenly become valuable if you just wait long enough. It's the decluttering equivalent of buying lottery tickets.

My grandmother Jean collected everything because you never knew what might become valuable. UFO magazines, religious pamphlets, books about alien encounters, conspiracy publications. She'd read articles about people finding valuable collectibles at garage sales and convince herself that everything she owned might be the next big discovery.

Jean's house was full of "potentially valuable" items that were worth nothing to anyone except antique dealers who specialized in convincing people their junk was treasure. She spent more money storing and organizing her collections than she would have made if she'd sold everything at its peak value.

Most things decrease in value over time, not increase. The few items that do become valuable are usually things that were rare or significant when they were made, not random household objects that everyone owned.

Excuse #8: "I can't afford to replace it."

This excuse assumes that you'll definitely need to replace something if you get rid of it. It's a way of avoiding the risk of needing something you no longer have, even when the probability of needing it is very low.

I kept a broken printer for two years because I "couldn't afford to replace it" if I needed to print something. Never mind that I hadn't printed anything in six months before it broke, or that I could print things at the library or office supply store for a fraction of what a new printer would cost.

The broken printer sat on my desk, taking up space and reminding me that I should either fix it or replace it. In the meantime, the few times I needed to print something, I found other solutions that worked fine and cost almost nothing.

If you can't afford to replace something, ask yourself if you can afford to keep storing it. The space it takes up has value, and the mental energy you spend thinking about it has a cost. Sometimes the cheapest option is to get rid of something and deal with replacing it if and when you need it.

The "Emotional Manipulation" Family of Excuses

These excuses use your feelings against you. They're designed to make you feel guilty about getting rid of things by suggesting that objects have feelings or that other people will be hurt if you don't keep their gifts.

Excuse #9: "It has sentimental value!"

This is the nuclear option of decluttering excuses because it's almost impossible to argue with. Who wants to be the person who throws away sentimental items? What kind of heartless monster doesn't value memories and emotions?

The problem is that "sentimental value" can be attached to anything if you think about it hard enough. That t-shirt from college has sentimental value because you wore it during finals week. That coffee mug has sentimental value because your coworker gave it to you. That random piece of paper has sentimental value because you wrote a note on it during an important phone call.

I realized I was using sentimental value as an excuse when I found myself getting emotional about a broken umbrella because it was the umbrella I'd carried on the day I got a job offer. The umbrella had no connection to the job offer, but my brain had created a sentimental story to justify keeping something that was obviously garbage.

Real sentimental value comes from genuine emotional connections, not from stories you make up to avoid throwing things away. If you have to think hard to remember why something is sentimental, it probably isn't.

Excuse #10: "It reminds me of [dead person]."

This excuse weaponizes grief to make you feel terrible about getting rid of anything connected to someone who's died. It suggests that getting rid of their belongings means forgetting them or disrespecting their memory.

After Jerry died, there was nothing to go through. I was 3,000 miles away. The social worker called, described the apartment, and asked what to do. I said donate everything. That was the estate settlement. No sorting, no sentimental archaeology, no deciding what to keep. There was nothing worth the logistics of retrieving, and I knew it.

I've thought about that phone call since. The decades of accumulation, the storage units, the apartment packed with pathways — reduced to a single instruction to a stranger. Not because I didn't care about my father. Because there was nothing in that apartment that represented him better than the call itself did. That's what the road to keeping everything leads to.

Dead people don't need their stuff. They're not watching to see if you keep their broken reading glasses or their collection of expired coupons. Keeping everything they owned doesn't honor their memory. It just clutters up your life with objects that make you feel sad.

Excuse #11: "It was a gift!"

This excuse assumes that getting rid of a gift is an insult to the person who gave it to you. It suggests that you're obligated to keep everything anyone has ever given you, regardless of whether you like it or have any use for it.

I had a shelf full of gifts that I didn't like, didn't use, and didn't want, but felt guilty about getting rid of. Decorative objects that didn't match my style, books about subjects that didn't interest me, kitchen gadgets I'd never use. All of them were "gifts," so I felt obligated to keep them.

The truth is that the gift was the act of giving, not the object itself. The person who gave you something wanted you to be happy. If keeping their gift doesn't make you happy, you're not honoring their intention by holding onto it.

Most people who give gifts don't keep track of whether you still have what they gave you. And if they do, that's their problem, not yours. You're not a storage facility for other people's generosity.

Here's what I noticed in my own audits: I was keeping objects from people who had been out of my life for decades. Someone gives you something in 1998, you lose touch by 2002, and in 2024 you're still housing their shopping decision out of loyalty to a relationship that ended twenty years ago. The obligation to the giver transferred to the object and just stayed there, unchallenged. The real question isn't 'was this a gift?' The real question is: does this have any value in my life right now? If the answer is no, it goes. The relationship it came from is not preserved by keeping the object. It already ended.

Excuse #12: "It's a family heirloom!"

This is the ultimate guilt trip excuse because it suggests that getting rid of something means betraying your entire family history. It elevates random objects to the status of sacred relics that must be preserved for future generations.

My parents elevated this to an art form. They'd drive into the desert specifically to collect purple glass electrical insulators. They hauled home a massive popcorn machine from the 1950s. They acquired antiques from swap meets and flea markets and declared everything a treasure. My father "borrowed" taxidermy specimens from the local university for his artwork — and never returned them. When his apartment was cleaned out after he died, there were dozens of them in various stages of decomposition. Family heirlooms, every one.

The problem with declaring everything a family heirloom is that it makes everything equally important, which means nothing is important. A real family heirloom is something with genuine historical or emotional significance to your family. It's not every object your relatives happened to own.

Most "family heirlooms" are just old stuff that nobody wanted to throw away. If your great-grandmother's china has been sitting in boxes in your basement for twenty years, it's not an heirloom. It's clutter with a story attached.

The "Other People" Family of Excuses

These excuses shift responsibility away from you by suggesting that other people need you to keep things or that society will benefit from your hoarding.

Excuse #13: "I'm saving it for my kids."

This excuse assumes that your children will want to inherit all the stuff you don't want to deal with. It's a way of postponing decluttering decisions by making them someone else's problem in the future.

Valerie saved everything for me: her books, her antiques, her collections, her random household items. She was convinced that I'd want all of it someday, even though I'd never expressed interest in any of it. When she died, I inherited their apartment and two storage units full of stuff that meant nothing to me but that she'd kept because she thought I'd want it.

Here's a radical idea: ask your kids what they want. Most of them will tell you they don't want your stuff. They have their own stuff, their own style, their own lives. They don't need to inherit your problems along with your belongings.

If you want to save something for your children, save one or two items that have real meaning, not everything you've ever owned. Your kids will thank you for leaving them memories, not storage units.

Excuse #14: "Someone could use this."

This excuse disguises hoarding as altruism. It suggests that you're keeping things not for yourself, but for the hypothetical someone who might need them someday. It's a way of feeling good about not making decisions.

I had boxes of clothes that didn't fit me but that "someone could use." Books I'd never read again but that "someone might enjoy." Kitchen gadgets I never used but that "someone would appreciate." All of this theoretical generosity was just an excuse to avoid the discomfort of getting rid of things.

If you really want someone to use something, donate it now. Keeping it in your closet doesn't help anyone. The longer you hold onto things while telling yourself someone else needs them, the more likely they are to deteriorate to the point where nobody can use them.

Excuse #15: "It's still good!"

This excuse confuses functional with necessary. Just because something still works doesn't mean you need to keep it. Just because something isn't broken doesn't mean it belongs in your house.

Valerie had kitchen appliances from the 1970s that were "still good." They worked fine, but they were ugly, inefficient, and took up cabinet space that could have held things she actually used. She kept them because throwing away something that still worked felt wasteful.

"Still good" doesn't mean "still useful to you." A coat that's still good but that you never wear isn't serving any purpose in your closet. A book that's still good but that you'll never read again isn't doing anyone any good on your shelf.

Excuse #16: "My [relative] would roll over in their grave."

This excuse uses dead people as enforcers of your clutter. It suggests that deceased family members are somehow monitoring your decluttering decisions and will be upset if you get rid of their things.

I've used the guilt excuse about my own accumulated junk. "I might need this someday." "I spent good money on that." The emotional version is the same mechanism — the object becomes a stand-in for the relationship or the person, and releasing it feels like a betrayal. It isn't. The relationship exists in memory, not in objects.

Dead people don't have opinions about your stuff. They're dead. They've moved on to whatever comes next, and it doesn't involve caring about whether you keep their old coffee maker.

Using dead relatives as justification for keeping clutter isn't honoring their memory. It's using their death as an excuse to avoid making decisions.

The "Practicality" Family of Excuses

These excuses make hoarding sound like responsible planning. They're dangerous because they appeal to your desire to be prepared and organized.

Excuse #17: "I don't have time to deal with it."

This excuse postpones decluttering decisions indefinitely by claiming that you're too busy to make them now. It suggests that there will be a perfect future moment when you'll have unlimited time to sort through everything.

I used this excuse for years to avoid dealing with boxes of papers, books, and random items that I'd moved from apartment to apartment without ever unpacking. I didn't have time to go through them, so they just sat there, taking up space and making me feel guilty about not dealing with them.

The truth is that you don't have time not to deal with clutter. Every day you keep something you don't need is another day you spend mental energy thinking about it, moving around it, and feeling bad about not dealing with it.

Making quick decisions about obvious clutter takes less time than moving it around for years while promising yourself you'll deal with it later.

Excuse #18: "I need to research its value first."

This excuse turns decluttering into an academic research project. It suggests that you can't get rid of anything until you've thoroughly investigated its potential worth, which conveniently takes forever and never gets done.

I had books sitting on my shelves for months while I "researched their value" on eBay and Amazon. I was convinced that some of them might be worth more than I thought, so I couldn't donate them until I'd checked every single title.

The research project never ended because there was always another book to check, another auction to compare, another price guide to consult. Meanwhile, the books sat there taking up space while I pretended I was being thorough and responsible.

If something is obviously valuable, you already know it. If you have to research whether something is valuable, it's probably not valuable enough to justify the time you're spending researching it.

Excuse #19: "I'll organize it better."

This excuse suggests that the problem isn't too much stuff, but inadequate organization. It promises that the right storage system will make everything manageable, so you don't need to get rid of anything.

Jerry believed that every organizational problem could be solved with better storage. He'd buy storage bins, shelving units, and pegboards to organize his collections instead of reducing them. The garage looked like a storage store showroom, but he still couldn't find anything because there was too much stuff to organize effectively.

Organization is useful for things you need and use. But organizing things you don't need is just creating a more complicated way to store clutter. No amount of organization will make unnecessary items necessary.

Excuse #20: "But look how much space it takes up!"

This is the weirdest excuse because it uses the problem as justification for not solving it. It suggests that because something takes up a lot of space, you can't get rid of it because... it takes up a lot of space.

I used this excuse to keep a large piece of furniture that I didn't like but that seemed too big to move. It was taking up half my living room, but getting rid of it would require renting a truck or hiring movers, which seemed like too much work.

Meanwhile, the furniture continued taking up half my living room for two more years. I spent more time and energy living around it than it would have taken to get rid of it. The space it occupied had a cost that I was paying every single day.

Large items that you don't want are exactly the items you should prioritize getting rid of. The space they free up is immediately noticeable and valuable.

Here's the question that exposes every excuse in this chapter for what it is: is this making my life better?

Not "might it make my life better someday." Not "was it useful once." Right now, today, in your actual life — does owning this thing give you something? Because if the honest answer is no, then every excuse you've generated for keeping it is just a story your brain invented to avoid the discomfort of letting go. The excuse sounds reasonable. But reasonable isn't the same as true.

You're alive. You have a limited number of hours. The things in your home that take up space, attention, and time without giving anything back are spending those hours for you, on their behalf, without your consent. Every excuse you accept for keeping them is a small vote for continuing that arrangement.

Breaking Free from Excuse Addiction

I have never met anyone who could generate excuses for keeping things faster than my friend Hector. He had a gift for it — a fluency that was almost impressive.

The leaf blower is the example I think about most. It had stopped working two years before I met him, and it was sitting in his garage taking up about four square feet of floor space.

When I asked why he was keeping it, he produced three separate justifications in under a minute.

First: "It was expensive." He'd paid $180 for it. Fair enough, except that the money was spent regardless of whether the leaf blower sat in the garage or went to the trash.

Second: "I might need it once I get it fixed." I asked when he planned to get it fixed. He'd been meaning to look into it. For two years.

Third, and this is where it got creative: "I've had it since we moved into this house." I said I didn't see what that had to do with anything. He said it felt like it was part of the house now.

Sentimental value. For a broken leaf blower. That he'd owned for four years and used for two.

The fascinating thing about Hector was that none of these excuses were conscious lies. He believed them as he said them. His brain was generating justifications in real time because letting go of things felt wrong, and the justifications were the mechanism for making it feel okay to keep them.

The leaf blower eventually went to the trash. Hector laughed about it later. But it took almost a year of pointing out the pattern every time I saw it before the excuses stopped being automatic.

Once you learn to recognize the pattern — the way the excuses stack up, the way one excuse fails and another appears immediately — you'll start catching yourself doing it too. Everyone does. The difference is noticing it.

The key to overcoming these excuses is to recognize them for what they are: your brain's way of avoiding the discomfort of making decisions and letting go. Every excuse sounds reasonable in isolation, but when you start using multiple excuses for the same item, you know you're just making up stories.

When you catch yourself using one of these excuses, ask yourself: "If I didn't own this item already, would I go out and acquire it today?" If the answer is no, the item doesn't belong in your life, regardless of how you acquired it or how long you've had it.

The goal isn't to get rid of everything you own. It's to reclaim the time, space, and attention your stuff is spending on your behalf without your permission. The "cost" language in this chapter isn't an argument for owning less. It's an argument for owning honestly. The things that genuinely add to your life aren't costing you — they're paying. The things sitting in your life through inertia, guilt, or a story you stopped believing are the ones running up the tab. Keep the first kind. Let the excuses protecting the second kind go.

Chapter 6: The Master Plan: How to Declutter (Without Losing Your Mind)

You've identified the dangerous stuff and learned to recognize your excuses. You understand the four piles and you've chosen your decluttering method. Now comes the part where most people completely screw everything up: the execution.

I've watched people start decluttering projects with the best intentions and end up making their homes look like a hurricane hit a storage unit. They pull everything out of every closet at once, get overwhelmed by the chaos they've created, and spend the next six months living in a disaster zone while promising themselves they'll "get organized" someday.

The problem isn't lack of motivation or good intentions. The problem is that most people approach decluttering like they're preparing for the Olympics when they should be training for a marathon. They try to do everything at once, burn themselves out in the first week, and then give up because the whole thing feels impossible.

Decluttering isn't a sprint. It's not even a race. It's more like learning to play a musical instrument: you start with simple songs and gradually work your way up to more complicated pieces. You don't sit down at a piano for the first time and expect to play Chopin.

Here's the master plan that will work, assuming you follow it instead of trying to improve it with your own "better" ideas.

Phase 1: Mental Preparation (Don't Skip This!)

Before you touch a single item, you need to get your head right. I know this sounds like therapy nonsense, but trust me on this. The biggest obstacles to successful decluttering aren't physical. They're mental.

First, you need to shift your mindset from "getting rid of stuff" to "choosing what deserves space in your life." This isn't just semantic wordplay. When you frame decluttering as getting rid of things, it feels like loss. When you frame it as choosing what to keep, it feels like control.

I learned this the hard way during my first major decluttering attempt. I spent the entire time feeling guilty and sad about everything I was throwing away. Every item felt like a small failure, a reminder of money wasted or opportunities missed. I was mourning my stuff instead of celebrating my progress.

The second time around, I approached it differently. Instead of focusing on what I was losing, I focused on what I was gaining: space, peace of mind, and freedom from managing things I didn't need. The same actions felt completely different when I changed my perspective.

Second, you need to set realistic expectations. This isn't a weekend project, and you're not going to transform your entire house in a month. If you've been accumulating stuff for years or decades, it's going to take time to sort through it all.

I see people get discouraged because they spend an entire Saturday working on one closet and feel like they haven't made any progress. But one closet is progress. One drawer is progress. One shelf is progress. The goal isn't to finish everything quickly. The goal is to make steady progress without burning yourself out.

Jerry and Valerie tried to declutter their house exactly once in the twenty years I knew them. They spent a weekend pulling everything out of every room, got overwhelmed by the magnitude of the project, and shoved everything back where it came from. Then they declared that decluttering "doesn't work" and never tried again.

They failed because they tried to solve a twenty-year accumulation problem in a weekend. It's like trying to lose fifty pounds in a month. Even if it were possible, it wouldn't be sustainable.

Third, you need to build your decluttering stamina gradually. Making decisions about your possessions is mentally exhausting. Decision fatigue is real, and it gets worse as the day goes on. If you try to make five hundred decluttering decisions in one day, the last hundred decisions are going to be terrible.

Start with fifteen-minute sessions. Set a timer and stop when it goes off, even if you're on a roll. It's better to maintain your energy and enthusiasm for weeks than to burn yourself out in one marathon session.

I used to think that stopping when I had momentum was stupid. If I was finally motivated to declutter, shouldn't I keep going until I ran out of steam? But I learned that momentum is like a muscle. If you overwork it, it needs time to recover. If you pace yourself, you can maintain it indefinitely.

Fourth, you need a support system. This doesn't mean you need to hire a professional organizer or join a decluttering support group. But you do need at least one person who understands what you're doing and why it matters to you.

The support person's job isn't to help you make decisions about your stuff. Their job is to remind you why you started when the process feels endless.

Phase 2: The Strategic Approach

Once your head is in the right place, you need to choose your strategy. There are two main approaches: room-by-room and category-by-category. Both work, but they work for different types of people and different types of clutter problems.

Room-by-room is better if you want to see immediate results and you're motivated by visible progress. You pick one room, work on it until it's completely decluttered, then move to the next room. The advantage is that you get the satisfaction of completing entire spaces. The disadvantage is that you might have the same type of item scattered across multiple rooms, making it harder to see how much you have.

I used the room-by-room approach for my first major decluttering because I needed to see progress. Having one completely organized room gave me motivation to tackle the next one. But I discovered that I had books in every room of my apartment, and I didn't realize how many books I owned until I started finding them everywhere.

Category-by-category is better if you have the same type of item scattered throughout your home and you want to make consistent decisions. You gather all your books from every room, deal with them all at once, then move on to clothes, then kitchen items, and so on. The advantage is that you can see the full scope of each category. The disadvantage is that your house might look worse before it looks better.

Valerie never tried the category approach. She never tried any approach. The clothes stayed in the closets, and more clothes came in, and eventually the closets couldn't close. That's the actual version of what happens when nobody ever does the category sort. It's less dramatic than a bed buried under clothing, but it's more honest.

Choose your approach based on your personality and your living situation. If you need to see quick wins and you can't handle having your entire house disrupted, go room-by-room. If you want to make consistent decisions and you can tolerate temporary chaos, go category-by-category.

Once you've chosen your approach, you need to set up your four-pile system in a place where it won't interfere with your daily life. You'll be living with these piles for weeks or months, so don't put them somewhere that will make your life miserable.

I made the mistake of setting up my piles in my living room because it had the most space. For two months, I had to navigate around boxes of stuff every time I wanted to watch TV or have friends over. It was a constant reminder that my decluttering project was taking over my life, making me resent the whole process.

The second time, I set up my piles in my bedroom because I could close the door and ignore them when I needed a break. It was less convenient for sorting, but it was much better for my mental health.

You also need to decide how you're going to handle the logistics of getting rid of things. Research donation centers in your area and find out their hours and requirements. Some places only accept certain types of items. Some require appointments. Some will pick up large items.

Figure out your selling strategy if you're planning to sell things. Are you going to use eBay, Facebook Marketplace, Craigslist, or something else? Each platform has different requirements and audiences. Don't wait until you have a pile of things to sell before you figure out how selling works.

Set up a system for the paperwork that comes with decluttering. You'll want to keep receipts for donations for tax purposes. You'll want to track what you're selling and for how much. You'll want to remember which pile certain items went into in case you need to find them later.

I know this sounds like a lot of preparation for what should be a simple process, but the preparation is what makes the difference between success and failure. People who skip the setup phase end up with their cars full of donation items that they drive around for months without dropping off.

One aspect of the strategic approach that often gets overlooked: what to do with the things you've decided to let go before they actually leave your home.

The staging problem is real. You sort things into the donate pile, and then the donate pile sits in a corner for three months because you haven't gotten to the donation drop-off. The sell pile fills up and the listings don't get made. The trash pile grows until it's too large for a regular trash day and the effort of dealing with it becomes its own obstacle.

Each category needs a logistics plan before you start sorting, not after.

For donations: identify your nearest drop-off location and its hours before your first session. Many areas have free pickup for larger volumes. The Salvation Army, Habitat for Humanity ReStore, and local furniture banks often pick up directly from your home. Book the pickup before you fill the pile, not after.

For selling: decide your platform — eBay for collectibles and specific-market items, Facebook Marketplace for local pickup of larger items, a consignment shop for clothing and small goods if you prefer not to manage individual transactions. Set a deadline. Items that haven't sold in thirty days move to donate. Don't let the sell pile become an indefinite holding zone.

For trash: be honest about volume. If you're doing a serious declutter, you will generate more trash than a regular pickup handles. Rent a dumpster, schedule a junk removal service, or plan multiple trips to a transfer station. The cost is real but the alternative — a trash pile that becomes an obstacle — is worse.

Phase 3: The Execution

The most common mistake I've seen people make when they finally decide to declutter is trying to do too much at once.

My friend Keiko had made two serious attempts before we talked. Both times, she'd pulled everything out of multiple rooms at once, spread it across every available surface, and then stood in the middle of the chaos feeling so overwhelmed that she'd shoved most of it back and declared herself a failure at decluttering.

This is not a failure of willpower or motivation. It's a failure of planning. You cannot make good decisions about hundreds of items simultaneously. Your brain doesn't work that way. Decision fatigue sets in faster than most people expect, and once it does, the default answer to every question becomes "keep it" — which is exactly where you started.

I told Keiko: fifteen minutes, one drawer. Set a timer. Stop when it goes off. Don't open a second drawer until the first one is completely done.

She thought I was joking. One drawer in fifteen minutes wasn't going to make any visible difference. She had entire rooms to deal with.

I said that was exactly the problem with her previous attempts. She was trying to solve everything at once, running out of energy before she could finish, and ending up worse off than when she started. One drawer finished was better than three rooms half-done.

She called me the next day. She'd done six drawers. Each one took about fifteen minutes. When she finished the first one and saw the result — actually saw a completed, organized drawer — the momentum was there for the next one.

The lesson isn't that small actions are all you can take. It's that small actions are how you build the confidence and momentum for larger ones. Start absurdly small. Finish completely. Move on.

Now you're ready to start making decisions about your stuff. But you're not going to start with the hardest decisions. You're going to start with the easy ones and build your confidence.

Begin with what I call the "practice round." Find the most obviously useless items in your house and get rid of them. Expired medications, broken electronics that you've been meaning to fix for years, clothes with holes or stains, books you hated the first time you read them.

The practice round serves two purposes. First, it gets you comfortable with the physical process of sorting things into piles. Second, it gives you some quick wins that prove you can do this without dying of regret.

My practice round involved going through my junk drawer and throwing away everything that was obviously garbage: dried-up pens, expired coupons, broken rubber bands, mystery keys that didn't open anything, instruction manuals for appliances I no longer owned. It took fifteen minutes and filled half a trash bag, but it made me feel like a decluttering genius.

After the practice round, move on to items that require slightly more thought but still have obvious answers. Clothes that don't fit, duplicates of things you only need one of, gifts you never liked, souvenirs from trips you'd rather forget.

Work your way up to the more difficult decisions gradually. Don't try to tackle your most sentimental possessions on day one. Save those for when you've built up your decision-making muscles and proven to yourself that getting rid of things won't kill you.

Use the 20-20 rule for items you're unsure about: if you can replace something for less than twenty dollars in less than twenty minutes, you don't need to keep it. This rule eliminates most of the "but what if I need it someday" anxiety because you know you can easily replace it if that magical someday ever arrives.

The 20-20 rule saved me from keeping a lot of random household items that seemed important but weren't. That extra can opener in case my main one broke? Replacement cost: five dollars, replacement time: five minutes. Those backup phone chargers for phones I didn't own anymore? Not worth the mental energy of storing them.

When you start feeling overwhelmed or indecisive, take a break. This isn't an emergency. The stuff isn't going anywhere. Come back to it when you're feeling fresh and clear-headed.

I learned to recognize the signs that I needed to stop: when I started keeping things because I was too tired to think about whether I needed them, when I started getting emotional about obviously useless items, when I started moving things from pile to pile without making real decisions.

The most underestimated enemy of the execution phase is perfectionism.

Perfectionism shows up as the need to do it right before you do it at all. You can't start decluttering the bedroom until you have the right storage containers to put things in. You can't deal with the kitchen until you know exactly what system you're going to use. You can't sort the papers until you have a filing system designed.

None of this is necessary. You can sort things into boxes on the floor. You can make keep-donate-trash decisions without knowing where the keep items will ultimately live. You can start before you have a plan for where everything is going, because the process of sorting will clarify the plan.

Done imperfectly is worth infinitely more than planned perfectly but never started.

The second enemy is the rescue reflex. This is the moment, usually about an hour into a sorting session, when you start pulling things back out of the donate pile. You've been making decisions for an hour. Decision fatigue has set in. Your brain is looking for ways to reduce the cognitive load, and the easiest way to do that is to start saying yes to everything.

Recognize the rescue reflex when it appears. It feels like sudden clarity — "wait, I might actually use this." It's not clarity. It's fatigue. When you feel the urge to rescue things from the donate pile, take a break. Drink some water. Come back in fifteen minutes. If you still want to rescue something after the break, fine. But most rescue impulses dissolve when the fatigue passes.

Tackling a large space — a garage, a basement, an attic — is a different problem than decluttering a drawer or a shelf, and it requires a different approach.

The mistake most people make is treating a large space as one problem. It isn't. It's thirty smaller problems stacked on top of each other. The garage isn't the project. The workbench is the project. The shelving unit along the back wall is a project. The boxes piled in the corner are a project. Break the space into zones before you touch anything, and work one zone at a time to completion before moving to the next.

Zone by function, not by area. The gardening tools are a zone. The sports equipment is a zone. The holiday decorations are a zone. Tools are a zone. Boxes labeled "miscellaneous" are their own category — treat them as a separate zone and work through them last, because they're usually the least organized and the most draining.

Time-box each session. A full Saturday in a garage typically produces worse results than five two-hour sessions over a few weeks, because decision fatigue sets in hard after about two hours and everything after that gets kept by default. Set a timer. When it goes off, finish the item in your hands and stop. Put everything in its designated pile — Keep, Donate, Trash, Sell — and close the door. Come back Thursday.

The "one zone finished" principle is the garage equivalent of the junk drawer approach from earlier in this chapter. You don't need to finish the whole garage to feel progress. You need to finish the workbench. That completed zone is evidence the process works, which makes starting the next zone easier.

For the mystery boxes — the ones labeled "misc" or not labeled at all that haven't been opened in over a year — apply the unopened box rule: if you can't remember what's in it and you haven't needed anything from it in a year, consider donating the box without opening it. One exception: boxes from significant life transitions — a deceased relative, a former home, a relationship that ended, a period you haven't fully processed. These deserve to be opened, even if the opening is hard. The story about Burt in Chapter 8 is a reminder that forgotten letters and photographs sometimes live in boxes you've been avoiding. The mystery box rule is for the bin of random household items, not for the last box from your mother's apartment.

Phase 4: Advanced Techniques

Once you've mastered the basics, you can use some advanced techniques to speed up the process and handle difficult items.

The one-touch rule: handle each item only once during your sorting session. Pick it up, decide which pile it goes in, put it in that pile, and move on. Don't pick things up multiple times to reconsider your decision. Trust your first instinct and keep moving.

The photography method: for items with sentimental value that you don't use, take a photo and then donate the item. You keep the memory without keeping the object. This works especially well for children's artwork, old greeting cards, and souvenirs.

I used the photography method for a box of cards and letters that my deceased wife had given me. I wanted to remember her words, but I didn't need to keep the physical papers. Scanning them into digital files gave me the content without the clutter.

The container method: for categories where you have too much stuff, choose a container that represents how much space you're willing to dedicate to that category. Keep only what fits in the container. This works well for books, DVDs, craft supplies, and other collections.

When I was decluttering my book collection, I decided that I was willing to dedicate one bookshelf to books I might read again. Everything that fit on the shelf stayed. Everything else went to donation. It forced me to choose my favorites instead of trying to keep everything.

The replacement strategy: when you buy something new, get rid of the old version immediately. New shirt means old shirt goes to donation. New kitchen gadget means old kitchen gadget gets donated. This prevents accumulation and forces you to make decisions when your enthusiasm for the new item is high.

The advanced techniques described in this chapter share a common principle: they reduce the number of active decisions you have to make during a session.

Decision fatigue is real, and it compounds quickly when you're handling emotionally charged material. Every time you pick something up and have to decide which pile it goes in, you spend a small amount of decision-making capacity. By the end of a long session, that capacity is depleted, and the decisions you make in that depleted state are reliably worse — you keep things you should donate, you rescue things from the donate pile, you feel overwhelmed by items that would have been easy decisions an hour earlier.

The one-touch rule, the photography method, the container method — all of these reduce decision load by either eliminating the decision entirely (one touch, one destination) or by pre-deciding the outcome before you start (the container constrains the decision to what fits). Use them when you feel the session starting to drag, when you notice yourself second-guessing decisions you already made, or when you're handling a category that you know from experience tends to create friction.

The most underused advanced technique is the most basic: stopping. Not every session needs to reach a natural conclusion. If you're tired, stop. If you're getting emotional and it's affecting your judgment, stop. If you've been going for more than two hours, stop regardless of how you feel. The stuff will still be there. Your decision-making capacity is the limited resource, not the time.

Phase 5: Maintenance and Prevention

The goal isn't just to declutter once. The goal is to stay decluttered. This requires building habits that prevent future accumulation and systems that make it easy to deal with new stuff as it enters your life.

The daily ten-minute pickup: spend ten minutes each day putting things back where they belong and dealing with any new clutter that has appeared. This prevents small messes from becoming big problems.

The monthly maintenance: once a month, do a quick sweep through your house looking for items that have outlived their usefulness. Deal with them immediately instead of letting them accumulate.

The one-in-one-out rule: for every new item that enters your house, one old item leaves. This keeps your total amount of stuff stable instead of constantly growing.

The entrance filter: create a system for dealing with things when they first enter your house. Mail gets sorted immediately. Shopping bags get unpacked and the bags thrown away. Gifts get evaluated and either kept or donated within a week.

The key to successful maintenance is making it automatic. You don't want to have to remember to do these things or decide whether today is a good day for maintenance. You want these habits to be as automatic as brushing your teeth.

I've been maintaining my decluttered space for three years now, and it's become effortless. I don't think about whether to keep things. I don't debate with myself about where things belong. I just follow the systems I've established, and my space stays organized without any drama.

The master plan works because it's based on building skills gradually instead of trying to do everything at once. You start with easy decisions and work your way up to harder ones. You start with short sessions and gradually increase your stamina. You start with simple systems and add complexity as you get more experienced.

Most importantly, you treat decluttering as a skill to be learned instead of a problem to be solved. Once you've learned the skill, maintaining a clutter-free life becomes easy. You know how to make decisions about your stuff quickly and confidently. You know how to prevent accumulation before it becomes a problem.

The master plan exists for one reason: to get you to the other side faster, with less burnout, so more of your life can be spent on something other than managing your accumulated possessions. Every phase of this plan is designed to reduce the time and attention your stuff demands so you can redirect it toward the life you're actually trying to live.

Your stuff will never again control your life because you'll have the tools to control your stuff.

Chapter 7: Room-by-Room Combat (Or: How Every Space in Your House Became a Hoarder's Paradise)

You've made it to the actual work part of this book. This is where we stop talking about decluttering in theory and start confronting the reality that every single room in your house has turned into a small-scale storage facility run by someone with questionable judgment. Namely, you.

Each room in your house has its own personality disorder. The kitchen thinks it's a Williams-Sonoma showroom. The bedroom believes it's a clothing museum. The garage has completely given up on its original purpose and now identifies as a warehouse for broken dreams and rusty metal objects.

I've been through this battle in every type of room, and I can tell you that what works for taming your kitchen's gadget addiction won't work for your bathroom's shampoo hoarding problem. It's like each room hired a different therapist and they're all giving conflicting advice.

But here's the thing: every room is supposed to have a job. When rooms stop doing their jobs and start moonlighting as storage units, your whole house becomes as dysfunctional as a reality TV family.

The Kitchen: Where Appliances Go to Die

I knew a woman named Rosario who had stopped cooking. Not because she didn't know how — she was a genuinely skilled cook who had once made elaborate Sunday dinners for her whole family. She'd stopped because her kitchen had become so cluttered with appliances and equipment that cooking felt like too much work before she even started.

When I went over and we counted, she had twenty-two small appliances on her counters and in her cabinets. A bread maker. Two blenders. A juicer she'd used twice. A pasta machine from a cooking class she'd taken in 2019. A waffle iron she'd bought because she made waffles once a year at most. An air fryer, an Instant Pot, a slow cooker, and a rice cooker — all four, all used occasionally, all competing for the same cabinet space.

She'd been ordering takeout three or four nights a week. At roughly sixty dollars a meal for a family of three, she was spending close to a thousand dollars a month on takeout that she didn't particularly enjoy, because the kitchen she loved cooking in had become too overwhelming to navigate.

We spent a Saturday afternoon going through everything. The rule was simple: if you used it in the past month, it stays. If you didn't, you need a specific occasion in the next month that requires it — not a hypothetical someday, an actual scheduled event. Everything else went.

She kept eight appliances. The other fourteen went to donation.

She cooked dinner that same night. She texted me a photo of it.

The clutter hadn't just taken up counter space. It had taken up her relationship with her own kitchen. Some clutter costs you money directly. This kind costs you the activities that make you feel like yourself.

The kitchen should be the simplest room to figure out. Its job is to help you turn raw ingredients into food and then clean up the mess afterward. That's it. Cook food, eat food, clean up. Even cavemen had this figured out.

Instead, modern kitchens have become appliance graveyards where perfectly good gadgets go to collect dust and guilt. Every surface becomes a monument to optimistic purchasing decisions and the triumph of hope over experience.

Valerie's kitchen was a perfect case study in how a functional space becomes a storage unit with a stove in it. She had accumulated enough small appliances to open a competing store to Bed Bath & Beyond. Every cabinet contained something she'd bought with the best intentions and used exactly once.

The bread maker that was going to save money and provide fresh bread for the family? Used twice, then promoted to "expensive countertop decoration." The pasta machine that was going to transform Tuesday nights into Italian culinary adventures? Buried under a pile of mail, probably plotting its revenge. The juicer that was going to revolutionize her health? Never made it out of the box because apparently assembling seventeen pieces just to drink vegetables isn't as appealing as it sounds on the infomercial.

My personal favorite was the food dehydrator she bought to "make healthy snacks." Three years later, I found it in the pantry still in its original packaging, next to a bag of Oreos. The irony was so thick you could have dehydrated it.

Here's what happens: you see an infomercial at 2 AM. Your sleep-deprived brain thinks, "Yes! This $39.99 gadget will finally transform me into the person who makes fresh pasta on weeknights!" You buy it. You use it once. You realize that making fresh pasta requires time, ingredients, and motivation that you don't possess. The gadget becomes a $40 reminder of your failure to become Italian.

The solution? Start with the appliance intervention. Pick up each gadget and ask yourself: "When was the last time I used this, and when will I realistically use it again?" If you can't remember the last time or can't imagine a specific future scenario that doesn't involve a personality transplant, it goes.

Don't fall for the "but it was expensive" trap. The money is already gone. Keeping the bread maker won't bring back the $79 you spent. It will just continue taking up counter space and making you feel guilty every time you buy bread at the store like a normal person.

Count your dishes. If you live alone and own seventeen coffee mugs, you might have a problem. Unless you're planning to host a coffee club for people with commitment issues, you probably need four mugs maximum. I know this because I had the seventeen-mug problem. I could have caffeinated a small book club without doing dishes for a week.

The junk drawer deserves special mention as your recommended starting point, especially if you don't know where to begin. It's the easiest decluttering decision you will ever make, because someone already made it for you. The drawer is labeled junk. You just have to agree with it. Everything in there is either useful and belongs somewhere else, or it isn't useful and belongs in the trash. There is no emotional archaeology required. No eleven-question audit. No grief. Just a drawer full of objects that have been waiting for you to acknowledge what they already know about themselves.

I once excavated a junk drawer that contained: fifteen dead batteries I was apparently running a hospice for, keys to locks that no longer existed, four broken pens, three working pens that I could have used at any point in the last two years if I'd known they were there, a birthday card from 2011, menus from restaurants that had closed, rubber bands that had fused into a single organism, and a small plastic thing whose purpose I have never been able to identify. Not a single item caused me any distress to throw away. I felt unreasonably good about myself for the rest of the afternoon.

Start with the junk drawer. Always. Clear it out, feel the satisfaction of one completed task, and let that carry you into the next thing. The emotional work comes later. The junk drawer is just practice.

Bedrooms: The Museum of Abandoned Identities

Bedrooms should be simple: a place to sleep and store the clothes you do wear. That's it. Sleep, get dressed, sleep some more. Even teenagers can handle this concept, though they choose not to.

Instead, most bedrooms become storage facilities for every version of yourself you've ever been or thought you might become. It's like a personality archive with a bed in the middle.

Jerry's bedroom was a perfect example. He had art supplies that had migrated from the garage into the house. Books he was going to read "when he had time." Boxes of items from previous moves that he still hadn't unpacked. And always, the sense that someday he'd get to all of it.

The space under the bed is especially dangerous because it's invisible storage. You can shove things under there and pretend they don't exist. It's like the witness protection program for objects you don't want to make decisions about.

I found a box under my bed that I hadn't opened in two years. When I finally looked inside, it was like archaeological evidence of poor decision-making: books I'd meant to read (but apparently not enough to keep them visible), clothes that used to fit (back when I had different eating habits), and random items I couldn't even remember packing.

The entire box was essentially garbage with sentimental value. I'd been sleeping above a time capsule of my own bad choices for two years.

The closet situation is where things get really psychological. Bedroom closets become museums dedicated to every version of yourself you've been for the past decade: Professional You (suits for jobs you no longer have), Athletic You (workout clothes from when you worked out), Social You (party clothes from when you went to parties), and Optimistic You (clothes that will fit "when you lose weight").

I had clothes representing at least four different people, none of whom were current me. I kept them because getting rid of them felt like admitting those versions of myself were permanently retired. Meanwhile, I wore the same five outfits repeatedly because they were the only clothes that fit both my body and my actual lifestyle.

When you're decluttering your closet, try everything on. I know this sounds like torture, but it's the only way to distinguish between clothes that fit your body and clothes that fit your fantasies. If something doesn't fit, it goes. If it fits but makes you feel bad about yourself, it goes. If it fits and looks fine but you never wear it because it doesn't feel like "you," it definitely goes.

The bedroom closet is where most people's decluttering efforts go to die, because it requires the most honest self-assessment.

Here's a method that cuts through the emotional noise: the reverse hanger trick. Turn every hanger in your closet so it faces the wrong direction — hook pointing toward you instead of away. Every time you wear something and put it back, hang it correctly. After six months, everything still facing the wrong direction is something you haven't worn in six months. Get rid of it.

This works because it removes the "but I might wear it" argument. You get six months of actual data. Not feelings, not intentions — data. The reverse hanger trick is unarguable.

For under-bed storage: if you're going to use it, make it intentional and labeled. A box labeled "extra bedding" that actually contains extra bedding is fine. A box labeled "misc" that hasn't been opened in two years is not storage — it's avoidance with a lid.

For the nightstand and dresser drawers: these are high-frequency areas where things accumulate fast. A weekly five-minute reset — everything that landed here without a purpose goes somewhere else — prevents the slow creep that makes drawers impossible to close.

Living Areas: The Decoration Trap

Living rooms are where good intentions about home decorating go to multiply into clutter. The goal is to create a space that looks magazine-worthy while still being functional for actual humans. This balance is where most people fail spectacularly.

Jerry and Valerie's living room looked like a museum exhibit called "Things That Looked Important at the Store." Every surface was covered with objects that had seemed necessary for a "finished" look but just created more surfaces to dust and navigate around.

Coffee tables became dumping grounds for magazines they never read, mail they needed to sort, remote controls for devices they no longer owned, and decorative items that served no purpose except to prove they were the kind of people who owned decorative items.

The bookshelf was genuinely tragic. It contained books they'd never read and probably never would read, but keeping them made the room look "intellectual." It was like set decoration for the life they thought they should have rather than the life they lived.

Want to put a drink down? First move the decorative bowl. Want to find the remote? Check under the stack of catalogs that arrived three months ago. Want to sit comfortably? First relocate the throw pillows that are too pretty to lean against.

The room looked "decorated," but nobody could live in it. It was a stage set designed to impress visitors who rarely came and didn't care about throw pillows anyway.

When you're decluttering living areas, ask yourself whether each item makes the space more functional or just more decorated. If you can't use your coffee table because it's covered with decorative objects, you don't have a coffee table. You have an expensive display stand that occasionally holds beverages.

Keep only decorative items that you genuinely enjoy looking at. If you have to dust something every week but don't get any pleasure from seeing it, you're basically paying rent to a decorative object that contributes nothing to your happiness.

The living room is the room most likely to be decluttered for the wrong reason: because guests are coming.

Decluttering-for-guests produces a specific kind of result: things get moved rather than dealt with. The pile from the coffee table gets shoved in a closet. The stack of mail gets put in a drawer. Everything looks clean. Nothing was actually decided.

Decluttering-for-yourself produces a different result. You're not trying to achieve the appearance of order for a few hours. You're trying to create a space that functions for your daily life. That means the things that live on your coffee table should be there because they belong there, not because they were moved there from somewhere else and never moved again.

The test for any decorative item in a living space: do you notice it and appreciate it, or has it become invisible from familiarity? Things that have become invisible aren't decorating your room.

They're just occupying it. Dust them once, notice whether you actually enjoy them, and let go of the ones that don't register.

Bathrooms: The Smallest Room with the Biggest Delusions

Bathrooms should contain only items you use for personal hygiene. This should make them the easiest rooms to organize, but bathrooms have a special talent for accumulating products that seemed essential at the store but turned out to be completely useless at home.

Medicine cabinets become graveyards for beauty products promising transformation but delivering disappointment. I once cleaned out a medicine cabinet that contained aspirin that expired during the Obama administration, sunscreen from a beach trip I'd forgotten I took, and enough different allergy medications to stock a small pharmacy.

Why did I keep allergy medicine that didn't work? Because I'd paid money for it, and throwing out "perfectly good" medicine felt wasteful. This is bathroom logic: keep everything because you paid for it, even if it makes you sneeze or gives you weird side effects.

The towel situation in most bathrooms is insane. I had eight bath towels for a one-person household. Eight. I was apparently prepared to host a swim team or go multiple weeks without doing laundry. My linen closet looked like a textile warehouse run by someone with trust issues about towel availability.

You need two towels per person: one to use while the other is being washed. Maybe three if you want a backup for emergencies. Any more than that is just hoarding terrycloth.

The same logic applies to shampoo. Count how many bottles you have open simultaneously. If you're currently maintaining relationships with five different shampoo brands, you might have a problem. Pick one. Commit to it. Let the others go find new homes where they'll be appreciated.

Garage/Basement/Attic: Where Dreams Go to Rust

The garage, basement, and attic have one thing in common that makes them harder to declutter than any room in the house: the absence of daily friction.

Every room you live in provides daily feedback. A cluttered kitchen makes cooking harder every day. A packed closet makes getting dressed harder every morning. The friction is immediate and continuous, which eventually motivates change.

The garage provides no friction. You can close the door. You can park in the driveway instead. The boxes in the basement can go another year without being opened. The attic doesn't care whether you visit it or not. These spaces are easy to ignore, which means the accumulation in them is often the oldest, the densest, and the most thoroughly forgotten.

The approach that works: treat these spaces as if they were rooms you use daily. Go in once a week even when there's nothing to do. This sounds unnecessary, but the regular presence prevents the gradual normalization that makes accumulated junk invisible. You stay familiar with what's in there. Things that are taking up space without purpose stay visible rather than fading into the background.

When you're actually decluttering these spaces, be honest about the category of "I might need this someday." This category is where most of the trouble lives. The holiday decorations you haven't used in five years. The furniture that doesn't fit anywhere but might be useful if you move someday. The boxes of papers you're keeping in case something comes up. Apply the same logic you'd apply to anything else: if you can't name a specific upcoming use, it goes.

These spaces are the final boss level of decluttering because they're out of sight and climate-controlled, making them perfect for storing items indefinitely. They're also where the most dramatic transformations happen because they often contain decades of accumulated evidence that you used to be different people with different interests.

Jerry's garage was a masterpiece of delayed decision-making dressed up as preparation. Every tool, every piece of outdoor gear, every broken appliance represented a project he was going to get to eventually. The raft was for the river trip he was always about to plan. The garden tools were for the garden that was perpetually one season away. The garage had become a physical manifestation of decades of "I'll use this when the time is right." The time was never right.

They moved from San Bernardino to Lake Arrowhead later in life. The San Bernardino house had the garage. The Lake Arrowhead house was different — no garage. Instead it had what's called a yankee cellar — half underground, half above, the kind of space that looks like a basement but breathes like a shed. My parents treated it the same way they treated every other space they ever occupied: as overflow storage for decisions they didn't want to make. Everything that didn't fit in the house went into the yankee cellar. When they finally abandoned that house in their seventies, they packed up everything they could carry. The heavy stuff — the pool table with its real slate bed, things too large or too costly to move — stayed behind. The rest came with them, because of course it did.

These spaces resist decluttering because they seem infinite. You can always find room for one more box, one more broken appliance, one more project you'll fix "someday." The problem is that someday has the same arrival schedule as the tooth fairy.

When you're tackling these spaces, be more honest than usual. If you can't remember what's in a box and you haven't needed anything from it in the past year, donate the entire box without opening it. I know this sounds extreme, but if you can't remember what's in there, it's not important to your current life.

The key is to resist turning these spaces into museums for your past selves. Just because you have room to store your college textbooks doesn't mean you should store your college textbooks. Just because the Christmas decorations fit in the attic doesn't mean you need to keep Christmas decorations that last saw daylight during the Bush presidency.

The universal question for every room, every space, every item in this chapter: is this earning its place in my life, or is it just occupying it?

Earning means it contributes something — function, beauty, joy, utility. Occupying means it's there through inertia, through the accumulation of small decisions not to deal with it. Your home is made up of rooms you live in. When those rooms are full of occupiers, you don't live in them — you navigate around them. That's not living. That's managing.

Universal Rules for Every Room

No matter which room you're attacking, these rules apply everywhere:

If you haven't used something in a year, you've broken up with it but just haven't made it official yet. Time to serve the eviction notice.

If something is broken and you haven't fixed it in six months, you're not going to fix it. You're just in denial about your repair skills and storage space.

If you have multiple versions of the same thing and only need one, keep the best one and let the others find new homes where they'll be the favorite instead of the backup.

If something makes you feel bad when you see it, why are you keeping it? Life is too short to be emotionally abused by your possessions.

If you're keeping something for a person you used to be or think you might become someday, you're running a storage facility for fictional characters. Focus on who you are right now.

Every room should serve your current life, not preserve evidence of your past lives or warehouse supplies for your hypothetical future lives. Your house should work for you, not against you. And if your stuff is controlling your living space, it's time to show it who's really in charge.

Chapter 8: The Psychology of Letting Go (Or: Why Your Brain is a Hoarder's Best Friend)

Welcome to the part of the book where we talk about feelings. I know, I know. You thought this was going to be a practical guide about getting rid of stuff, not a therapy session. But here's the uncomfortable truth: your brain is sabotaging your decluttering efforts, and it's been doing it so long that you probably think the voice in your head saying "but I might need this someday" is the voice of reason.

It's not. It's the voice of a hoarder who has taken up residence in your skull and convinced you that keeping seventeen extension cords is "being prepared" instead of "being crazy."

Getting rid of your stuff is going to mess with your head in ways that Instagram decluttering influencers don't warn you about. They show you the pretty "after" photos, but they don't tell you about the 2 AM panic attacks when you suddenly remember the broken toaster you threw out three months ago and convince yourself you've made a terrible mistake.

Your possessions aren't just objects sitting around taking up space. They're emotional support systems, security blankets, trophies, insurance policies, and tiny monuments to every version of yourself you've ever been or hoped to become. When you start getting rid of them, you're not just cleaning house. You're performing surgery on your identity with a garbage bag and no anesthesia.

Here is the more precise version of what's actually happening: objects absorb the emotional context of how they were acquired and what they were associated with. An object bought during a depressive episode carries that episode. An object given by someone who harmed you carries that harm. An object from a period of your life you'd rather not revisit keeps that period present in your daily environment whether you are consciously thinking about it or not.

Your home becomes a physical record of your emotional history. Some of that history is good — objects connected to genuine love, joy, and meaning belong there, and keeping them is not hoarding, it's living. But mixed in with those objects are others that carry damage. Every day you walk past them, something in your nervous system registers it. The accumulation of those small exposures is the low hum of bad feeling that people living in cluttered homes often describe without being able to name it.

The flip side is equally true: removing those objects removes the exposure. Not the memory — you keep the memory regardless. But the daily reminder stops. The low hum stops. That is why one button from the wrong person's clothing can produce a week of relief. The button was delivering a small dose of harm every time it was seen. Remove the button, the dosing stops. It is that literal.

No wonder most people make it through one closet and then give up. Their brain starts screaming "WHAT ARE YOU DOING? WE NEED THAT STUFF!" and they decide maybe living with clutter isn't so bad after all.

The Stories Your Stuff Tells About You (All of Them Are Fiction)

Every item in your house comes with a story. Not the boring story about where you bought it or how much it cost, but the elaborate fiction you've created about why you absolutely cannot live without it. These stories are masterpieces of creative writing. Your brain has had years to perfect them, and they're so convincing that you believe them yourself.

Take Jerry's collection of outdoor equipment. He had an entire garage bay dedicated to gear for activities he'd pursued once or planned to pursue someday. A raft from a single river trip twenty years earlier. Gardening tools for a garden that was always one season away from happening. Camping equipment for a camping enthusiast who had camped maybe three times in his adult life. He couldn't get rid of any of it because "I might use it" and "you never know."

This was the "someday" fantasy in physical form. If Jerry was ever going to take that camping trip, he wasn't going to wish he'd kept the tent he bought in 1987. He was going to buy new gear, because thirty-year-old camping equipment doesn't work properly and he knew it. But getting rid of it meant admitting the trips weren't going to happen.

The outdoor gear represented an identity. Jerry was the kind of man who could go camping, go rafting, grow a garden. Getting rid of the equipment felt like admitting he wasn't that person and probably never would be. The gear wasn't preserving his potential. It was preserving his anxiety about not living up to it.

I had the same problem with my photography equipment graveyard. I'd gone through a phase where I was convinced I could build a portrait and wedding photography business. I bought cameras, lenses, tripods, lighting equipment, and enough accessories to outfit a small studio. I spent probably $4,000 on gear that was going to pay for itself once I started booking those lucrative portrait sessions.

The portrait sessions never materialized. Neither did the wedding gigs. I did eventually find my footing as a photographer — documenting renaissance festivals, masquerade balls, bellydance events, the Tournament of Roses — but that work didn't require the studio setup I'd bought. The lighting gear and portrait equipment sat in the closet making me feel like a failure for years before I finally sold it.

For years, I kept all that equipment because getting rid of it would mean accepting that I'd wasted $4,000 on a fantasy. But keeping it wasn't making the money come back. It was just taking up space and making me feel bad about myself every time I needed to find a winter coat.

When I finally sold everything, I got maybe $1,200 for gear that had cost me $4,000. It hurt, but it was $1,200 more than I had when the equipment was sitting in my closet reminding me of my failed artistic ambitions. More importantly, I got my closet back and stopped hauling expensive equipment I never used from one apartment to the next.

The sunk cost problem goes deeper than economists usually describe it, because it isn't just about money. You can have a sunk cost in time, in identity, in relationships.

The hobby you spent years developing before you lost interest — the sunk cost there isn't the equipment. It's the years you invested. Letting go of the equipment feels like invalidating the investment of time and effort, which feels like admitting those years were wasted.

The relationship you were in that produced objects — gifts, photographs, shared purchases — that are now painful to look at. The sunk cost there is the emotional investment. Keeping the objects feels like honoring what was real about the relationship. Getting rid of them feels like pretending it didn't happen.

The version of yourself you spent years cultivating — the athlete, the artist, the adventurer — whose equipment still occupies your spare room. The sunk cost there is identity. Letting go of the equipment means accepting that this version of yourself isn't current anymore, which can feel like loss even when it's actually just change.

In all of these cases, the logic of sunk costs applies: the investment has been made. It doesn't change based on what you do with the objects. The time you spent on the hobby is part of your history regardless of whether you keep the equipment. The relationship was real regardless of whether you keep the gifts. You were that person regardless of whether the gear is still in your closet.

Keeping the objects doesn't preserve the investment. It just keeps a reminder of it in your physical environment — and whether that reminder is helpful or harmful is a genuine question worth asking honestly.

The Sunk Cost Fallacy Has Moved Into Your House

Economics professors love to talk about the sunk cost fallacy in terms of business investments and stock market decisions. But the sunk cost fallacy doesn't live on Wall Street. It lives in your house, paying rent by convincing you to keep expensive mistakes instead of cutting your losses.

You keep the exercise bike that you rode exactly three times because you paid $600 for it. You keep the hobby supplies for the crafting phase you lost interest in after two weeks because you spent $300 on materials. You keep the formal dinnerware that you've used once in five years because it was expensive and "good quality."

The money is gone. The bike didn't magically become worth $600 again because you let it serve as a clothing rack for another six months. The craft supplies aren't going to inspire you to become a quilting enthusiast just because they're taking up space in your spare room. The fancy dishes aren't improving your life while they're hidden in a cabinet making you feel guilty about eating off paper plates.

Valerie was the queen of sunk cost hoarding. She kept a bread maker that she used twice because "it was expensive." She kept a pool table that took up an entire room because "we paid good money for it." As far as I know it stayed in their house when they finally abandoned it — it had a real slate bed, so moving it would have required professional movers and considerable expense. She kept a set of china that came out of storage exactly once in fifteen years because "it's too nice to get rid of."

The bread maker cost her $89 in 1997. By 2015, she had spent more on storing it and moving it from house to house than the original purchase price. She was essentially paying interest on a broken appliance to avoid admitting she'd made a bad purchase eighteen years earlier.

The Museum of All Your Past Selves

One of the cruelest tricks your brain plays is convincing you to maintain a museum dedicated to every person you used to be. These aren't necessarily bad memories. They're monuments to previous versions of yourself, and getting rid of them feels like erasing your own history.

I had boxes of elaborate costumes from my masquerade ball phase. Victorian gowns, Renaissance doublets, steampunk accessories, and enough period-appropriate jewelry to outfit a small theater company. I'd spent months researching historical accuracy, bought custom-made pieces, and even learned to walk properly in a corset (don't ask).

These weren't Halloween costumes from a discount store. These were museum-quality reproductions that cost hundreds of dollars each. I'd attended maybe a dozen events over three years, and for those magical evenings, I was transformed into someone elegant, mysterious, and sophisticated. Someone who belonged in a different century where people appreciated artistry and craftsmanship.

Then life moved on. The events became less frequent, my interest in elaborate historical costuming faded, and the costumes got packed away in storage boxes. But I couldn't get rid of them because they represented creativity, artistry, and a connection to history. Getting rid of them felt like admitting that I was just another boring modern person with no appreciation for beauty or craftsmanship.

But keeping the costumes wasn't making me more artistic or sophisticated. They were just reminding me that I used to do something interesting and didn't anymore. Every time I moved, I had to carefully pack and unpack boxes of delicate historical costumes that I hadn't worn in years. I was paying moving companies to transport the fossilized remains of my Renaissance fantasies.

The "What If" Warehouse in Your Head

The most persistent voice in the hoarder's chorus is the one that whispers "but what if I need it someday?" This voice has convinced people to keep paint cans with two inches of dried paint, boxes of computer cables for devices that were discontinued during the Obama administration, and enough plastic containers to stock a restaurant supply store.

The "what if" voice feels logical and responsible. It seems smart to keep items that might be useful in hypothetical future scenarios. Why get rid of that extra extension cord when you might need it for something someday? Why throw out those magazines when you might want to reference an article eventually? Why donate that broken appliance when you might fix it if you ever get around to learning how?

Jerry's garage was a perfect example of "what if" thinking taken to its logical extreme. He had outdoor equipment "in case" he decided to take up an activity again. He had paint cans from every room he'd painted in the past fifteen years "in case" he needed to do touch-ups. He had broken appliances "in case" he learned how to fix them. Raft equipment for a river that wasn't going anywhere. Gardening tools for soil that stayed bare.

The garage looked like a hardware store that had been hit by a tornado and then abandoned. Jerry couldn't find anything when he needed it because everything was buried under layers of "what if" supplies. When he needed a screwdriver, he usually gave up looking and bought a new one rather than excavate his tool collection.

The "what if" supplies weren't making Jerry more prepared. They were making him less functional. He was spending time and energy managing hypothetical future needs while ignoring his actual current needs, like being able to park his car in the garage.

The Guilt Industrial Complex

A friend of mine named Burt lost his mother three years before we talked about it. She'd left behind a full apartment's worth of belongings — furniture, clothes, decades of accumulated possessions — and Burt had dutifully sorted through enough of it to clear the apartment, then packed the rest into boxes, put some in his basement, and rented a storage unit for the overflow.

Three years later, he was paying $175 a month to store boxes he'd never opened. He knew roughly what was in them. Books his mother had loved. Clothes he couldn't bring himself to donate. Kitchen items he didn't need but felt guilty getting rid of. Things that had been hers and were therefore, somehow, still her.

He wasn't avoiding the storage unit out of laziness. He was avoiding it because opening those boxes meant making decisions, and making decisions meant the process was actually happening, and the process actually happening meant it would eventually be over — and over meant she was really gone in some final, practical way he wasn't ready for.

I didn't tell him to just deal with it. That's useless advice for someone in that position. What I suggested instead was a reframe.

Instead of asking "what can I get rid of," ask "what actually represents her?" What, if someone who'd never met her found it, would help them understand who she was?

He went through everything with that question. It took him two full weekends. He came out with one medium-sized box. Her favorite cookbook with her handwritten notes in the margins. Three photographs he hadn't known existed. A small piece of jewelry. A letter she'd written to him that he'd forgotten he had.

The hardest object wasn't any of those. It was a coffee mug — plain white, nothing special, the kind you'd find in any kitchen. She had drunk her coffee from it every morning for as long as he could remember. He held it for a long time. It didn't represent her in any way he could explain to a stranger. It just held the specific weight of a thousand ordinary mornings he'd never have again. He kept it. It sits on his shelf next to the cookbook.

Everything else went. The storage unit closed. The basement boxes were gone.

He told me later that the box on his shelf felt more like her than the full storage unit ever had. The volume of stuff hadn't been honoring her memory. It had just been deferring a decision. When he finally made it, what was left was actually her.

Guilt is the emotion that keeps more clutter in houses than sentiment, fear, and laziness combined. Guilt about wasting money, guilt about being ungrateful, guilt about hurting someone's feelings, guilt about contributing to environmental destruction. Your stuff has formed an alliance with your conscience to convince you keeping everything is the moral choice.

Gift guilt is the most powerful weapon in the clutter army. Someone gave you that decorative bowl, that picture frame, that book you'll never read. Getting rid of it feels like slapping the giver in the face and announcing that their thoughtfulness was wasted on your ungrateful soul.

Valerie had accumulated enough guilt-driven gifts to stock a small gift shop. Coffee mugs with inspirational sayings that didn't inspire her, decorative items that didn't match her style, books on topics that bored her to tears, and clothes that fit neither her body nor her personality. She kept all of it because getting rid of any item felt like telling the giver that their gift wasn't good enough.

This is emotional blackmail disguised as gratitude. The purpose of a gift is to make you happy. If a gift isn't making you happy, it's not serving its purpose. Keeping it out of obligation isn't honoring the gift or the giver. It's turning your house into a storage facility for other people's shopping mistakes.

Environmental guilt is another favorite trick. You can't throw that perfectly good item in the trash because it will end up in a landfill. You can't donate it because it's too worn out for someone else to want. You can't sell it because it's not valuable enough to bother with. So you keep it, feeling virtuous about not contributing to waste while your house slowly transforms into a personal landfill.

Here's the reality check: that item is waste. Whether it's waste in your house or waste in a landfill doesn't change its fundamental nature. At least in a landfill, it's not taking up space in your living room and making you feel bad about yourself every time you see it.

The Breakthrough Moment (When the Crazy Voice Finally Shuts Up)

The breakthrough moment — the point where the resistance substantially drops and the process starts to feel like forward motion rather than effort — happens at different times for different people, but it happens.

For some people it's the first time they see a cleared surface. The visual evidence that the process actually works. The kitchen counter that's been buried under stuff for three years, suddenly visible. The closet that closes properly for the first time in memory. The empty shelf where forty boxes used to be.

For some people it's financial. The moment they cancel the storage unit and realize they're saving $175 a month on stuff they never looked at. The eBay sale that converts a forgotten box of items into actual money. The realization of how much the accumulation has been costing in dollars, not just in space.

For some people it's emotional. The session where they finally deal with a box they've been avoiding for years — a dead relative's things, or items from a painful period — and realize that dealing with it felt better than dreading it had felt. That the anticipated pain of letting go was worse than the actual pain. That on the other side of the hard box was something lighter. That's what happened when I finally finished going through Claudia's things. I'd spent a year dreading the last boxes. When I opened them, the dread was larger than the actual pain. After, I felt something I hadn't expected: relief that I'd finally let myself know what was in there.

For some people the breakthrough is social. They invite someone over for the first time in years. The shame that had been quietly driving their social withdrawal dissolves when there's nothing to be ashamed of anymore.

You don't know which kind of breakthrough will be yours until it happens. But it will happen, and when it does, the whole project shifts.

Breaking Free from the Hoarder in Your Head

The key to getting past the mental obstacles is to change the stories you tell yourself. Instead of asking "what if I need this someday," ask "what is keeping this costing me right now?" Instead of thinking about the money you spent in the past, think about the money you could make by selling things. Instead of focusing on what you're losing, focus on what you're gaining.

Start with the obviously useless stuff. The items that are clearly broken, clearly outdated, or clearly taking up space without providing any value. Build momentum with wins that don't require much emotional heavy lifting.

Then move to the items with simple stories. The exercise equipment you don't use, the clothes that don't fit, the gadgets that turned out to be disappointments. Practice letting go of things that you can logically justify getting rid of.

Save the sentimental stuff for last. Once you've developed your decluttering muscles on easier items, you'll be stronger for the emotional wrestling matches.

Remember: you're not just getting rid of things. You're getting rid of the mental burden of managing things. You're trading the weight of ownership for the freedom of space. You're firing the hoarder who has been running your house into the ground and taking back control of your own life.

The stories your possessions tell about who you are or who you might become are fiction. The only story that matters is the one you're living right now. Make sure your stuff supports that story instead of drowning it in clutter.

Chapter 9: Digital Decluttering (Your Computer is Also a Hoarder)

Congratulations! You've made it through the physical world of clutter and now you think you're done. You've conquered the kitchen gadgets, bedroom clothes museums, and garage archaeological sites. You're feeling pretty good about yourself, aren't you?

Well, sit down. We need to talk about your other house. The digital one. The one that lives inside your computer, phone, tablet, and any other device that connects to the internet. Because while you were busy getting rid of your physical junk, your digital life has been quietly turning into the electronic equivalent of Jerry's garage.

Your computer is a hoarder. It's been collecting files, photos, emails, and apps with the same enthusiasm that Valerie collected kitchen gadgets. The only difference is that digital clutter doesn't take up physical space, so you can ignore it for years without tripping over it.

But digital clutter is still clutter. It slows down your devices, wastes your time, clutters your mental space, and makes finding anything about as easy as locating a specific cable in Jerry's "what if" collection. You've just moved your hoarding problem from the physical world to the digital world, where it can multiply exponentially without anyone noticing.

Time to clean house. Again. But this time, the house is made of pixels and poor file management decisions.

The Desktop Disaster Zone: When Your Computer Screen Looks Like a Hoarder's Living Room

Let's start with your desktop. You know, that screen you see when you turn on your computer? The one that's supposed to show a nice wallpaper image but instead looks like a digital version of a hoarder's living room?

If you have more than twenty items on your desktop, you have a problem. If you have files named "New Document," "Untitled," "Copy of Copy of Final Version REAL," and "USE THIS ONE," you have a bigger problem. If you have so many files on your desktop that you can't see your wallpaper, you have officially recreated Jerry's garage in digital form.

My own computer desktop was a masterpiece of digital dysfunction at its worst. I had hundreds of files scattered across my screen like confetti from a very boring party. Photos, documents, shortcuts to programs I'd forgotten I installed, and multiple versions of the same document with names like "Final Version REAL" and "USE THIS ONE." I had Macs, PCs, and even a MicroVAX at various points — and each migration left behind digital sediment layers that never got cleaned up.

The digital desktop problem is the same psychology as a cluttered physical surface — everything lands there because it's the easiest place to put something temporarily, and temporary becomes permanent. Unlike Jerry's garage, which at least had the excuse of physical space filling up, a digital desktop can expand indefinitely. Which means it does.

My download folder was even worse. It contained every file I'd ever downloaded across multiple computers going back years. Software installers for programs I'd never used, PDF files I'd opened once, photos that people had emailed me. I treated the download folder like a junk drawer with infinite capacity. Everything went in with the assumption I'd organize it later. Later never came.

Email Hoarding: Why You Don't Need Every Receipt from 2003

If your desktop is the digital equivalent of Jerry's garage, your email inbox is the digital equivalent of Valerie's junk mail collection. Except worse, because email multiplies automatically and never stops coming.

Email inboxes are the digital equivalent of a hoarder's junk mail pile, with one crucial difference: the mail never stops coming and takes no physical space, so there's no natural pressure to address it. I've seen inboxes with tens of thousands of unread messages — newsletters, promotional emails, notifications from apps never opened again. The accumulation is invisible until you go looking for something important and can't find it.

Most people's email habits are like running a filing system designed by someone with organizational disorders. They keep everything because deleting feels wasteful, but they never organize anything because organizing feels overwhelming. The result is digital filing cabinets stuffed with the electronic equivalent of expired coupons and junk mail.

The email subscription problem is insidious. Every time you buy something online, sign up for something free, or show the slightest interest in anything, you get added to seventeen different mailing lists. These companies treat your email address like a valuable commodity to be traded, sold, and shared with anyone wanting to send you messages about things you don't want.

The result is an inbox that fills up with digital junk mail faster than you can delete it. You're basically running a personal post office for companies that want to sell you stuff, and you're doing it for free while letting them clutter up your digital life.

Most people have email relationships with companies they don't remember engaging with, for products they don't use, in categories they're not interested in. It's like having pen pals who only write to ask for money.

The most effective email strategy most people will ever implement is a single rule applied consistently: unsubscribe from every mailing list that sends you something you delete without reading.

This sounds obvious. It isn't practiced. Most people delete promotional emails for years without ever unsubscribing, because each individual deletion takes two seconds and feels easier than the thirty seconds required to unsubscribe. The math doesn't work. If a company sends you two emails a week that you delete without reading, unsubscribing saves you roughly an hour and forty minutes over a year. Per mailing list. Most people are on dozens.

The one-week unsubscribe exercise: for one week, every promotional email you delete, unsubscribe first. Just that week. The list you're maintaining will shrink dramatically.

For the existing backlog: the two-year rule is a reasonable starting point for bulk deletion, but a more aggressive approach works for most people. If you haven't opened or searched for something in a year, it can go. The fear that something important is buried in there almost never proves true — and if it does, most important things can be reconstructed from other sources.

Photo Management Hell: 47 Blurry Pictures of the Same Sunset Aren't Memories

Digital photography has turned everyone into accidental hoarders. Remember when taking photos required actual film that cost money to develop? You thought carefully before pressing the shutter button because each photo had a real cost attached to it.

Now photos are free, unlimited, and automatic. Your phone takes pictures when you don't mean to, saves multiple versions of the same shot, and encourages you to document every sandwich, sunset, and slightly amusing sign you encounter.

The result is photo libraries that make a hoarder's filing cabinet look organized and manageable. I have 23,000 photos on my phone alone — and that's not counting the serious photography work. Twenty-three thousand. I could look at a different photo every day for sixty-three years and still not see them all.

Most of these photos are garbage. Accidental shots of my pocket, blurry pictures of things I don't remember photographing, seventeen different versions of the same mediocre sunset, and enough food photos to start a very boring cooking blog.

I have photos of meals I ate five years ago. Why? What did I think I was going to do with a picture of Tuesday's lunch? Start a historical archive of my eating habits? Show future generations what avocado toast looked like in 2019?

The real problem isn't the storage space (although 23,000 photos take up a lot of room). The real problem is that having too many photos makes the good ones impossible to find. When you have hundreds of photos from every vacation, event, and random Tuesday, the special moments get buried under digital debris.

It's like keeping every piece of mail you've ever received and then wondering why you can't find your birth certificate when you need it. The important stuff gets lost in a sea of unimportant stuff that you never bothered to throw away.

The photo problem requires a different approach than the email problem because photos carry genuine emotional weight. You can't just bulk-delete a decade of photos the way you can bulk-delete promotional emails.

What you can do is establish a curation habit going forward and a triage system for the backlog.

Going forward: after any event, trip, or occasion, take thirty minutes to go through the photos before they join the archive. Delete the blurry ones, the duplicates, the accidental shots. Keep the ones that actually capture something. This thirty-minute investment prevents a month's worth of photos from becoming an indistinguishable mass of images you'll never look at.

For the backlog: don't try to process everything at once. Pick one period — one trip, one year, one event — and deal with that first. A folder of two hundred photos from a trip you took four years ago is manageable. Your entire photo archive is not.

The goal isn't to have fewer memories. It's to be able to find the good ones. A photo library with three thousand well-selected images is more useful than one with forty thousand undifferentiated ones.

App Addiction: You're Not Going to Use That Fitness Tracker App

Your phone is like a small computer you carry around with you. Which means it's also like a small hoarder's paradise that fits in your pocket. Most people's phones contain more apps than Valerie had kitchen gadgets, and they're used about as frequently.

I have 127 apps on my phone. I use maybe fifteen of them regularly. The rest are like digital versions of Jerry's broken extension cords — things I downloaded with good intentions that now just take up space and occasionally make me feel guilty about my lack of follow-through.

There's the fitness app that was going to track my workouts and help me get in shape. I used it for exactly three days before remembering that I don't like working out and prefer sitting on the couch. But I keep the app because deleting it feels like admitting defeat.

There's the meditation app that was going to help me find inner peace and mindfulness. I opened it once, listened to a five-minute guided meditation, and decided that sitting quietly with my thoughts was more terrifying than useful. The app is still there, silently judging my lack of spiritual development.

There's the budgeting app that was going to help me manage my finances and stop wasting money on unnecessary purchases. This is ironic, since I spent $9.99 on the app and then never used it. It's like buying an expensive diet book and then eating pizza while reading about portion control.

Most people have entire folders full of apps they've never used, games they played once, and utilities downloaded for specific situations that never arose again. The same psychology as Jerry's outdoor gear — acquired for a specific purpose, used once or never, kept because getting rid of it feels wasteful.

The apps sending notifications are problematic. They turn your phone into a device constantly interrupting you with information you didn't ask for about activities you're not doing. It's like having a personal assistant whose only job is to remind you about all the things you're not accomplishing.

Social Media Archaeology: Deleting Evidence of Who You Used to Be Online

Social media platforms are like digital museums dedicated to preserving every version of yourself you've ever been, whether you want them preserved or not. Facebook remembers your political opinions from 2008. Twitter has screenshots of your jokes that weren't funny. Instagram contains photos of your questionable fashion choices and ill-advised haircuts.

The problem with social media is that it creates a permanent record of temporary thoughts and feelings. That angry post you wrote about your job in 2012? Still there. The relationship status updates from the relationship that lasted three weeks? Still there. The photos from that party where you thought wearing a fedora was a good idea? Definitely still there.

I went through my Facebook timeline recently and found posts that made me cringe so hard I nearly pulled a muscle. There were political rants that seemed important at the time but now read like the digital equivalent of shouting at clouds. There were check-ins at restaurants that closed years ago. There were photos tagged by friends of events I'd completely forgotten attending.

Social media creates a weird form of digital hoarding where other people contribute to your collection without your permission. Friends tag you in photos you don't like, at events you'd rather forget, with people you no longer speak to. It's like having a house where anyone can walk in and leave their stuff without asking.

The photo tagging situation is problematic. You can delete your own embarrassing photos, but you can't delete the embarrassing photos that other people took of you and posted without permission. You're basically dependent on your friends' judgment about what makes you look good, which is a terrifying dependency given most people's approach to photography.

Then there's the issue of old comments and conversations that seemed hilarious at the time but now read like evidence of poor judgment and questionable humor. Internet culture moves so fast that jokes from five years ago seem like they were written by different people with completely different values and sensibilities.

The social media problem has a practical component that most decluttering advice ignores: you can't fully control what's on the internet about you.

What you can control is your own output. Going back through your oldest posts and deleting or hiding the ones that don't represent you accurately, the ones that were written in anger, the ones that reflect views you no longer hold, the ones that could be misread by someone who doesn't know you — this is digital decluttering in its most literal form.

The process doesn't need to be comprehensive or exhaustive. You're not trying to build a curated highlight reel. You're trying to remove the stuff that actively misrepresents you or that you'd be embarrassed by if anyone looked closely.

A practical approach: set aside two hours once. Go back to the beginning of your oldest account. Scroll forward. Delete or archive anything that makes you wince. Don't overthink it — if you'd be uncomfortable with a new employer or a new relationship seeing it, remove it. You're not erasing your history. You're editing it to reflect who you actually are rather than who you were at your worst or most impulsive.

The ongoing practice: before you post anything, ask whether you'd be comfortable with it being seen out of context in five years. This one question eliminates a significant percentage of social media clutter before it's created.

The digital purge has a different emotional character than the physical purge, and it's worth being prepared for that difference.

Physical stuff carries memory in a tactile, immediate way. Holding an object surfaces the feelings associated with it. This makes the physical purge emotionally intense but also emotionally clear — you know what you're feeling and why.

Digital stuff carries memory differently. It's mediated through screens, through file names, through the abstract presence of things you've forgotten you have. The emotional intensity tends to come in sudden bursts — you stumble on a folder of photos from a relationship that ended badly, or a document from a particularly difficult professional period, or messages from someone who is no longer alive. The rest of the time it feels administrative.

This means the digital purge requires a different kind of pacing. You can't necessarily predict when you'll hit something emotionally significant, so you can't front-load the hard work the way you might with physical stuff. Go at a pace that allows you to stop when you need to without feeling like the whole session was derailed.

Deleting digital items is permanent in a way that donating physical items isn't. If you donate something physical and regret it, there's a nonzero chance of finding a replacement. If you delete a digital file without a backup, it's gone. For anything with genuine emotional significance — photos, correspondence, documents connected to important life events — consider an archiving step before deletion. A folder labeled "archive" that you don't look at but know is there is a reasonable compromise for things you're not ready to permanently delete.

For everything else — the thousands of ordinary emails, the duplicate photos, the outdated files — delete without ceremony. They were never as important as the keeping-everything habit made them feel.

Your digital life makes the same demand as your physical life: everything you keep requires something from you, even if you can't see it.

A cluttered inbox consumes attention every time you open it. Ten thousand unorganized photos means the ones that actually matter are buried where you'll never find them. Apps you don't use interrupt you with notifications about activities you're not doing. The digital version of clutter does the same thing as the physical version — it claims space in your life without giving anything back.

You're alive and your time is finite. The same logic that applies to your garage applies to your hard drive.

The Digital Purge Strategy: Deleting Your Way to Sanity

I had a colleague named Nadia who had 47,000 emails in her inbox. Not archived — in her actual inbox, unread and unorganized, going back eleven years. The number itself was almost impressive. She'd never deleted anything, never unsubscribed from anything, never organized anything into folders. Everything that had ever arrived was still there.

When I asked her why, she said she was afraid there was something important buried in there. An email from years ago with a confirmation number she might need. A document someone had sent her that she might want to reference. Something.

I asked when she'd last searched for something in those 47,000 emails and actually found something useful she hadn't been able to get any other way.

She thought about it for a while.

She couldn't think of a single time.

The emails weren't a resource. They were an anxiety. The possibility of something important being buried in there was keeping her from deleting any of it, even though in practice she could never find anything when she needed it precisely because there were 47,000 of them.

We sat down and did a bulk select on everything older than two years. 38,000 emails. She hovered over the delete button for a long moment.

I said: if there's something important in there from three years ago that you haven't needed in three years, you probably don't need it now.

She deleted them.

Nothing bad happened. She didn't lose anything she needed. She didn't miss a critical email from 2019. What she did gain was an inbox she could actually navigate, and the low-level anxiety about the buried important email went with the emails themselves.

Digital clutter creates exactly the same psychological weight as physical clutter. The 47,000 emails weren't taking up visible space, but they were taking up mental space every time she opened her inbox. Clearing them was a relief she hadn't expected.

The good news about digital decluttering is that it's easier than physical decluttering in some ways. You don't have to worry about donating files or finding new homes for your old emails. You just delete them, and they disappear forever.

Old devices sitting in drawers are a specific category of digital clutter that combines physical mess with digital risk.

That old phone from four upgrades ago isn't just taking up drawer space. It probably still contains your old accounts, messages, photos, and personal information — even if you've "switched" to a new phone. Factory resetting a device before disposal is essential, and factory resetting isn't always sufficient for older devices where data recovery tools can reconstruct wiped storage.

The proper approach: for phones and tablets, back up anything you want to keep to your current device or cloud storage, perform a factory reset, then disable your accounts from the device's settings specifically. For computers, wipe the hard drive using dedicated software rather than just deleting files. For hard drives you're not going to reuse, physical destruction is the most reliable option.

The practical reality is that most people have two or three old phones in a drawer right now. None of them have been properly wiped. All of them contain accounts, messages, and personal information that creates risk. This takes about thirty minutes per device to address and eliminates a genuine security problem.

Start with the obviously useless stuff. Desktop files that you can't remember creating, downloads that you never opened, photos that are clearly accidents, apps that you haven't used in over a year. Build momentum with easy decisions before tackling the emotional stuff.

Then move to the duplicates and near-duplicates. You don't need seventeen versions of the same document. You don't need five slightly different photos of the same thing. You definitely don't need multiple copies of software installers for programs you're never going to reinstall.

Email is the easiest place to start because most of it is obviously garbage. Newsletter subscriptions for stores you don't shop at, promotional emails for services you don't use, notifications from apps you've deleted. Delete everything older than two years unless it's truly important. If you haven't needed it in two years, you're not going to need it.

For photos, be selective about quality. Blurry photos aren't memories — they're just blurry photos. If you wouldn't print it and put it in a physical photo album, you don't need to keep it in your digital photo album either.

Social media requires a different approach because you can't delete other people's contributions to your timeline. But you can untag yourself from photos you don't like, delete your own posts that make you cringe, and adjust your privacy settings to prevent future embarrassment.

The key is to remember that digital space isn't infinite, even though it feels like it is. Every file you keep makes your devices slower and your digital life more cluttered. Every app you don't use is taking up space that could be used for apps you do use. Every old email is making it harder to find new emails that matter.

Chapter 10: Maintaining Your Sanity (How to Stay Decluttered)

Congratulations! You've successfully decluttered your house, defeated your psychological attachment to broken toasters, and even cleaned up your digital life. You're feeling pretty good about yourself right now. Your surfaces are clear, your closets are functional, and you can find things when you need them. You've achieved the impossible: a clutter-free existence.

Now comes the hard part: staying that way.

Because here's what nobody tells you about decluttering: it's not a one-time event. It's not like getting your appendix removed, where you do it once and never have to think about it again. Decluttering is like dieting, exercising, or maintaining a healthy relationship — it requires ongoing effort, constant vigilance, and the willpower to resist temptation when it comes knocking at your door with a special offer.

Your stuff is going to try to come back. It's going to sneak in through online shopping, gift-giving relatives, and your own temporary lapses in judgment. One day you'll wake up and realize that your kitchen counter has somehow accumulated three coffee mugs, a pile of mail, and something called a "spiralizer" that you bought at 2 AM because the infomercial was very convincing.

Jerry and Valerie never developed any systems. They never tried to maintain. The stuff came in and never left. Learn from what actually happened to them, not a cautionary tale I made up — they ended up destitute, abandoned their house, moved to a small subsidized apartment fifty miles away, and somehow managed to bring all their possessions with them anyway.

The One-In-One-Out Rule: Simple Math That Works

The most effective system for preventing clutter accumulation is also the simplest: for every new item that enters your house, one old item has to leave. Buy a new shirt? Donate an old one.

Acquire a new kitchen gadget? Get rid of one you don't use. Bring home a new book? Find an old one to pass along.

This is basic inventory management. Your house has finite space, and pretending otherwise is how you end up with Jerry's garage situation.

The one-in-one-out rule forces you to make conscious decisions about everything you bring home. You can't just add new things to your existing collection and hope everything will fit. You have to choose what stays and what goes, which makes you think about whether you really need that new item or if you're just shopping out of boredom.

Jerry never followed this rule. He followed the "one-in-seventeen-in" approach, where buying one new piece of outdoor gear somehow justified keeping all the old gear plus acquiring more "just in case." The garage looked like a sporting goods store run by someone with severe organizational issues and unlimited storage optimism.

Valerie had the same problem with kitchen gadgets. She'd buy a new coffee maker but keep the old one "as a backup." She'd get a new set of pots but keep the old ones "for camping" (they never went camping). She'd acquire a new blender but keep the old one "for smoothies" (she never made smoothies).

The result was kitchen cabinets stuffed with redundant appliances and gadgets that served no purpose except to make finding anything impossible. She had three coffee makers, two blenders, and enough cooking utensils to equip a restaurant kitchen, but she couldn't find a can opener when she needed one.

The one-in-one-out rule would have prevented this accumulation by forcing Valerie to choose between old and new instead of keeping everything. When you have to give something up to get something new, you think more carefully about whether the new thing is better than what you already have.

This rule works for everything: clothes, books, electronics, decorative items, tools, hobby supplies, and anything else that tends to multiply when you're not paying attention. The key is to apply it consistently, not just when you remember or when things start getting cluttered again.

The one-in-one-out rule sounds simple. It's harder to practice than it sounds because the moments when it matters most are the moments when you're least likely to apply it.

You're excited about a new purchase. You want to enjoy it. The last thing you want to do at that moment is go find something to get rid of. So you don't. The new thing joins the collection. The old things stay. The total grows.

Making the rule automatic requires removing the decision from the moment of acquisition. The way to do this is to decide before you buy, not after. Before you bring a new kitchen gadget home, ask yourself: what am I getting rid of to make room for this? If you can't name it, reconsider the purchase. This isn't about being restrictive. It's about being honest with yourself that space is finite and accumulation is a choice.

For gifts and things that come in without being purchased — holiday presents, hand-me-downs, items people give you because they're decluttering their own homes — the rule applies equally. Something comes in, something goes out. The logistics of this can be handled through the donation bag that lives in your closet: the item going out doesn't have to leave the same day, but it needs to be designated.

Monthly Maintenance Purges: Richard's System for Staying Ahead

Even with the one-in-one-out rule, stuff has a way of sneaking back into your life. Mail accumulates on counters, clothes pile up on chairs, and random objects migrate from their designated homes to wherever you happened to set them down. This is normal. The trick is to catch the accumulation before it becomes overwhelming.

I do a monthly maintenance purge on the first Saturday of every month. It takes about two hours, and it prevents small accumulations from becoming big problems. I go through each room with a donation bag and a trash bag, looking for items that have outlived their usefulness or found their way into places where they don't belong.

The monthly purge isn't about major decluttering. It's about maintenance. Like getting regular oil changes for your car or cleaning your gutters before they overflow, monthly purges prevent small problems from becoming expensive disasters.

During each monthly purge, I ask myself three questions about every questionable item: Have I used this in the past month? Is it in the right place? Do I need it, or am I keeping it out of habit? (These are maintenance questions, different from the sorting questions in Chapter 3 — here the goal is to catch drift, not process the whole house.)

Most items caught in the monthly purge are things that seemed important when I acquired them but turned out to be useless in practice. Books I thought I'd read but never opened. Gadgets that seemed clever but weren't practical. Clothes that fit my fantasy self but not my actual lifestyle.

The monthly purge also catches gifts I felt obligated to keep but don't want, purchases I made during temporary enthusiasms that have since faded, and items that served a purpose in the past but are no longer needed.

Recognizing Early Warning Signs: When "Just This Once" Becomes "Just Like Jerry and Valerie"

It starts with "just this once." Just this once, I'll leave these papers on the kitchen counter instead of filing them. Just this once, I'll put these clothes on the chair instead of hanging them up. Just this once, I'll buy this gadget even though I don't really need it.

"Just this once" is the gateway drug to full-blown clutter accumulation. Every hoarder started with "just this once" and gradually normalized keeping everything, buying everything, and putting off decisions about everything.

Jerry's outdoor equipment collection started with "just this once." He kept the raft because "you never know," then bought camping gear because "we might go someday," then added gardening tools because "I've always wanted a garden." Twenty years later, he had a garage full of equipment for an outdoor life he'd mostly never lived.

Valerie's kitchen gadget addiction followed the same pattern. She bought one unnecessary appliance because it was "on sale," then another because it "might come in handy," then another because she was already "collecting kitchen tools." Eventually, her kitchen looked like a Williams-Sonoma store run by someone who never cooked.

The early warning signs of clutter re-accumulation are usually visible on surfaces. Kitchen counters, dining room tables, coffee tables, and bedroom dressers are like canaries in the coal mine for household organization. When these surfaces start accumulating random objects, it's a sign that your organizational systems are breaking down.

Other warning signs include buying duplicates because you can't find the originals, creating "temporary" piles instead of deciding where things belong, shopping for storage solutions instead of reducing what you own, making excuses for things you don't use, feeling overwhelmed when you walk into any room, and avoiding certain areas of the house entirely because dealing with them feels impossible.

The key is to catch these warning signs early and address them immediately, rather than waiting until they develop into major problems. A small accumulation on your kitchen counter is easy to deal with. A house full of accumulated junk requires months of work and significant emotional energy.

The warning signs of re-accumulation are worth memorizing, because they appear before the problem becomes visible.

The first warning sign is almost always invisible to the person experiencing it: you stop noticing what's accumulating. When you first decluttered, every new item entering the house felt conscious — a deliberate choice about what belongs. Over time, as the home feels organized and manageable, that vigilance relaxes. Things start appearing without being decided about. The landing zone by the door fills up. The kitchen counter gains objects. A pile forms on the bedroom chair.

This isn't failure. It's the normal entropy of a lived-in home. The question is how quickly you catch it.

The second warning sign is the return of avoidance. When you stop going into certain areas of your home because they've become uncomfortable to deal with, that's the same mechanism that created the original problem. Catch it early. The area you're avoiding now is easier to address than it will be in six months.

The third warning sign is the re-emergence of excuses. "I'll deal with this later" for specific items. "I might need this" for things that clearly don't belong. "I don't have time right now" as a recurring response to accumulation. These are the same cognitive patterns that created the original clutter. When you hear them in your own head, treat them as an alarm.

The monthly check described elsewhere in this chapter is specifically designed to catch all three of these warning signs before they compound. One hour once a month is significantly easier than several weekends once a year.

The annual purge is more than just maintenance. It's a yearly honest assessment of whether your home still matches your life.

Life changes faster than most people's accumulation patterns do. You change jobs, relationships, locations, interests. Your children grow up and move out. You age into different physical capabilities and different priorities. The things that served your life five years ago may not serve it now — and if you're not doing a thorough annual review, the gap between what you own and who you currently are quietly widens every year.

A useful structure for the annual review: go through the house with three questions. What has my life become this year that it wasn't last year? What has it stopped being? What did I acquire in the past year that hasn't earned its place?

The first question surfaces new needs — spaces that should be reconfigured, equipment that's actually missing, changes in how you use rooms. The second question surfaces things that belong to a chapter that's closed. The third question catches the year's accumulation before it becomes entrenched.

This isn't a full declutter. It's a tuning. It keeps the gap between your life and your home from growing wide enough to require another major overhaul.

The Annual Big Purge: Spring Cleaning That Doesn't Suck

Even with monthly maintenance and careful attention to warning signs, an annual big purge is necessary for most people. This is like an annual physical exam for your house — a comprehensive review of everything you own to make sure it's still serving your current life.

I do my annual big purge in January, when the holidays are over and I'm motivated to start the new year with a clean slate. The timing works well because the holidays usually bring an influx of new stuff (gifts, decorations, food), which means I need to make room and reassess what I'm keeping.

The annual purge is more thorough than monthly maintenance. I go through every closet, drawer, cabinet, and storage area with the assumption that everything is guilty until proven innocent. I pull everything out, evaluate each item individually, and only put back the things that serve my current life.

This is when I catch the items that have been hiding in the back of closets, the books I've been meaning to read for three years, the clothes that fit but make me feel bad about myself, and the hobby supplies for hobbies I've outgrown.

The annual purge is also when I reassess my organizational systems. Are my storage solutions working? Do I have too much stuff for the space I have? Are there categories of items that keep accumulating despite my best efforts?

Jerry and Valerie never did annual purges. They used the holidays as an excuse to acquire more stuff, then stored the excess wherever they could find space. The accumulation continued until they couldn't afford their house anymore, disappeared into a subsidized apartment fifty miles away without telling anyone, and brought everything with them anyway. The pattern followed them to the end.

The annual purge prevents this kind of accumulation by forcing you to regularly evaluate everything you own and make conscious decisions about what to keep. It's like an annual subscription renewal for your possessions - everything has to justify its continued presence in your life.

The single biggest source of re-accumulation for most people isn't gifts or hand-me-downs or things that sneak in through the back door. It's shopping.

Most shopping that generates clutter isn't driven by need. It's driven by boredom, by stress, by the hedonic hit of acquisition, by sales that create artificial urgency, by the low friction of online purchasing that puts things in your cart at 11 PM when your decision-making is at its worst.

Understanding this changes the maintenance strategy. You can't maintain a decluttered home while continuing the shopping patterns that created the clutter in the first place. The maintenance work isn't just about managing what comes in — it's about changing why things come in.

A practical audit: for thirty days, note every non-essential purchase and what triggered it. Not to judge yourself but to see the pattern. Most people find they're shopping in response to a fairly small set of triggers — specific emotional states, specific times of day, specific contexts. Once you see the pattern, you can interrupt it more deliberately.

The replacement strategy described elsewhere in this chapter handles the mechanics: one in, one out. The trigger audit handles the psychology: understanding why you're bringing things in is the upstream intervention that makes the one-in-one-out rule easier to maintain.

The three early warning signs described above have a common thread: they all involve a return to default behavior.

Default behavior for most people, shaped by the same consumer culture and the same psychological patterns that created the original clutter, is to accumulate. Acquisition feels natural. Letting go requires effort. Without active systems, the default wins.

This is why the warning signs matter more than they might seem. A pile on the kitchen counter isn't just a pile on the kitchen counter. It's evidence that the default is reasserting itself — that the effort required to maintain the cleared state has, in some small area, stopped happening. Left unaddressed, that one pile becomes the new normal for that surface, which slightly lowers the threshold for other surfaces, which six months later looks like the original problem.

The monthly check isn't about finding dramatic accumulation. Most months there won't be any. It's about keeping the threshold high — maintaining the expectation of cleared surfaces so that clutter never has the chance to normalize itself again.

Think of it like physical health maintenance. You don't wait until you're seriously ill to see a doctor. You do the regular checkups that catch small problems before they become large ones. The monthly declutter check is the equivalent — a low-cost regular practice that prevents the expensive crisis.

Building Habits That Stick

My friend Clarence called me frustrated about two years after a major declutter that had gone really well. He'd been through the whole process — multiple sessions, four piles, donated three truckloads, got his garage back, got his spare room back. For about six months he described it as life-changing.

Now the spare room was a dumping ground again. The garage was getting there. His wife was annoyed. He was annoyed.

"It didn't work," he said.

I told him it had worked. It worked for six months. The problem wasn't that decluttering didn't work. The problem was that he'd treated it as a one-time event rather than a practice.

He hadn't done anything to prevent the accumulation from returning. No one-in-one-out rule. No monthly check. No system for dealing with stuff as it came in. He'd done the surgery and then gone back to the habits that had required the surgery in the first place.

This is the most common mistake people make after a successful declutter. The declutter becomes the story — the dramatic transformation, the before-and-after — and the maintenance feels anticlimactic, so it doesn't happen. But maintenance is the whole game. The declutter is just the reset.

Clarence did a second pass — faster this time, because the accumulation was only two years deep rather than ten — and this time he set up the systems. Monthly check on the first Saturday. One-in-one-out on anything coming into the house. A donation bag in the closet that goes to the car when it's full.

He's been maintaining for three years now. He told me the monthly check takes about an hour and feels routine, like any other household task. It stopped feeling like a chore once the house stopped feeling like a problem.

The goal of all these systems — one-in-one-out, monthly purges, annual reviews — is to build habits that prevent clutter accumulation without requiring constant willpower or massive time investments.

Good organizational habits are like good health habits. They're easier to maintain than to restart. It's easier to spend ten minutes a day keeping your house organized than to spend an entire weekend decluttering a house that's gotten out of control.

The key is to make the habits as simple and automatic as possible. Don't create complicated systems that require perfect execution. Create simple systems that work even when you're tired, distracted, or not feeling motivated.

For example, I have a "landing zone" by my front door where I put things that need to be dealt with - mail to be sorted, items to be returned, things that belong in other rooms. This prevents random objects from migrating throughout the house and gives me a centralized location for quick daily maintenance.

I also have a "donation bag" in my closet where I add items throughout the month. When I try on clothes that don't fit or don't make me feel good, they go directly into the donation bag instead of back into the closet. When the bag is full, it goes to charity.

These habits work because they're simple, automatic, and built into my daily routine. I don't have to remember to declutter or set aside special time for organization. The habits handle the maintenance automatically, which prevents accumulation from becoming a problem.

The alternative is the Jerry and Valerie approach: ignore everything until it becomes overwhelming, then feel guilty about the mess but not motivated enough to deal with it, then continue ignoring it until it becomes someone else's problem.

The best organizational systems are the ones you maintain without thinking about them.

This sounds like a simple insight but it has real design implications. A system that requires you to remember to do it will eventually fail. A system that requires you to make decisions every time you use it will develop friction and get abandoned. A system that requires special supplies or dedicated spaces that don't fit naturally into your existing routine won't last.

The landing zone works because it's a single location with a single rule: things that enter the house and don't have an immediate destination go here, and nothing stays here more than a week. One location. One rule. No categorization required.

The donation bag works because it's always in the same place and the action is immediate: item in hand, bag is there, item goes in the bag. No separate trip, no separate decision about what to do with it later.

The one-in-one-out rule works because it builds the letting-go decision into the acquiring decision, which is the moment of highest motivation. You want the new thing. The old thing leaving feels like the price of getting the new thing, which is psychologically easier than deciding to let something go when you have nothing to gain from it.

Design your systems around your actual behavior patterns, not your aspirational behavior patterns. If you're not someone who files paper immediately, don't design a system that requires immediate filing. Design a system with a designated holding spot and a once-a-week filing session. The system that acknowledges how you actually behave is the one that persists.

Maintenance isn't housekeeping. It's protecting the life you've reclaimed.

The decluttering work you've done freed up time, space, and attention that was previously going toward managing stuff you didn't need. Maintenance is the practice of keeping it that way — of refusing to let accumulation quietly reclaim the ground you've taken back. Every monthly check is an assertion that your life is more important than your stuff.

Don't be Jerry and Valerie. Build systems that work even when you're not at your organizational best. Your future self will thank you, and you'll never have to live through another major decluttering project again.

Chapter 11: Life After Clutter (What to Do with All This Space)

Welcome to the other side. You've successfully decluttered your house, developed systems to keep it that way, and now you're standing in rooms that look like the rooms they were supposed to be. Your kitchen counter is visible. Your closets have breathing room. You can walk through your garage without playing three-dimensional Tetris with boxes and broken appliances.

This is what normal people call "having a functional house," but if you've been living like Jerry and Valerie for years, it probably feels like you've moved into a fancy hotel where everything is suspiciously clean and organized.

You might be experiencing some mild panic. Where did all your stuff go? What are you supposed to do with all this empty space? How are you supposed to fill the time you used to spend looking for things, moving things around, and feeling guilty about things you never used?

Don't worry. This is normal. You've just discovered what your house was like before it became a storage facility for your abandoned dreams and impulse purchases. This is what architects had in mind when they designed rooms with specific purposes instead of general-purpose dumping grounds.

Now comes the fun part: figuring out what to do with a house that works for you instead of against you. Spoiler alert: it's going to change your life in ways you didn't expect.

Rediscovering Your Home: Who Knew You Had Hardwood Floors?

The first shock of living in a decluttered house is discovering features you'd forgotten existed. That beautiful hardwood floor that's been hiding under piles of magazines for the past five years? It's back. The dining room table you could never use because it was covered with mail, projects, and random objects? You can eat dinner on it now. Revolutionary.

Jerry and Valerie's dining room table hadn't been used for eating in over a decade. It had become a horizontal filing system for everything without an obvious home: bills, magazines, mail, small appliances, craft supplies, and enough random objects to stock a small garage sale. They ate dinner in the living room while watching television, using their dining room as an expensive storage shelf.

The same transformation happened in my own living room. Once I cleared away the decorative items that served no purpose, the books stacked three deep on fifteen bookshelves, the electronics from computers I no longer owned — I discovered I had a comfortable space. One I could actually use. It had been there all along.

At my worst, I had a three-bedroom apartment where every room served as storage. The living room held bookshelves — fifteen of them, books stacked two and three deep on each shelf. Movies, tech equipment, computers I'd replaced but kept "just in case." It took half a dozen purge campaigns over years to get it down to something functional.

The psychological impact was bigger than I expected. Having clear surfaces and organized shelves — seven bookshelves now, books sitting loose with room to breathe — changed how the space felt to be in. Not a storage facility I happened to sleep in. An actual home.

The Mental Health Benefits: Why Decluttering is Cheaper Than Therapy

Living in a cluttered environment creates constant low-level stress you don't notice until it's gone. Every cluttered surface is a visual reminder of unfinished tasks, poor decisions, and things you need to deal with but haven't. Your house becomes a three-dimensional to-do list that follows you everywhere and never gets shorter.

When you declutter, you don't just remove physical objects. You remove psychological burdens. Every item you get rid of is one less thing to clean, organize, maintain, worry about, or feel guilty about. Your mental load gets lighter along with your physical space.

People who do declutter often describe this effect. The mental energy consumed by living in a cluttered environment is easy to miss because it becomes the baseline. You stop noticing the low hum of anxiety generated by surrounding yourself with things you feel guilty about, haven't dealt with, or don't want. Until it stops. Jerry never experienced that relief. Neither did Valerie or Jean. None of them ever cleared anything. The contrast I can offer is my own.

My own bedroom at worst had computers, boxes of books, and equipment from hobbies I'd abandoned stacked against every wall. Clearing it out changed how I slept. A room that's just for sleeping turns out to be much better for sleeping than a room that's also trying to be a storage unit, an office, and a hobby space.

The decluttering also reduced procrastination. When my workspace was cluttered and disorganized, starting any project felt overwhelming because I had to clear space before I could begin. The friction of getting started was so high that I'd put off projects for months. With a clean, organized workspace, starting became straightforward.

The tools were where they belonged. The workspace was ready to use. The projects I'd been avoiding for months got done in an afternoon. The environment had been sabotaging my productivity without my realizing it.

The mental health benefits of a decluttered home are real enough that researchers have studied them specifically.

A 2010 study published in the journal Personality and Social Psychology Bulletin found that women who described their homes as cluttered had higher levels of cortisol throughout the day than women who described their homes as restful. The cortisol levels didn't just spike when they were in the cluttered space — they stayed elevated. The home environment was affecting their stress hormones across the entire day.

Separate research on the relationship between clutter and depression has found consistent correlations: people living in cluttered homes report more symptoms of depression and anxiety than people in organized spaces, even when controlling for income, personality type, and other factors. The researchers were careful to note that causality runs both ways — depression can cause clutter, and clutter can worsen depression — but the relationship is real regardless of the direction.

What this means practically: decluttering isn't just an aesthetic improvement. It's an environmental intervention with measurable psychological effects. You're not just making your home look better. You're changing the chemical environment you live in.

One of the more surprising benefits people report after decluttering is discovering that they actually have taste — specific preferences about how things look and feel and function — that had been invisible underneath the accumulation.

This makes psychological sense. When your home contains objects from every phase of your life, purchases made under every kind of emotional pressure, gifts you kept out of obligation, things acquired without much thought at all — there's no coherent signal coming through. You can't hear your own preferences because they're drowned out.

When you remove everything that isn't genuinely yours — everything that represents who you used to be or thought you should be or received without wanting — what's left tells a clear story. It turns out you have consistent color preferences. Consistent aesthetic sensibilities. Things you reliably find beautiful versus things you find merely acceptable. You might not have been able to articulate these before, but you recognize them when you can finally see them.

This matters practically because it changes how you shop. Knowing what you actually like means buying things you'll keep and use rather than things that seemed like a good idea in the store. It means fewer impulse purchases that end up in the next donate pile. It means a home that feels coherent rather than accumulated.

It also matters personally. For many people, the process of decluttering is the first time they've asked themselves what they actually want, as opposed to what they should want or what they used to want or what someone else wanted them to want. The stuff was obscuring the answer. The answer was always there.

Finding Your Style: When You Can See What You Own

One unexpected benefit of decluttering is discovering your real taste in things. When your house is cluttered with accumulated objects from decades of impulse purchases, gifts you felt obligated to keep, and items you bought for imaginary future selves, it's impossible to tell what you genuinely like.

Clutter obscures your personal style the same way too many voices obscure a conversation. You can't hear your own preferences when they're drowned out by the noise of everything else you own. When you remove the excess, your actual taste becomes visible.

I had the same problem with my book collection. Three-bedroom apartment, fifteen bookshelves, books two and three deep on every shelf. A lot of those books were books I thought I should own — technical manuals, serious literature, business books promising success. When I was honest about what I actually read and reread, the collection went from overwhelming to manageable. Seven bookshelves. Books loose. Room to find what I'm looking for.

Jerry kept art supplies and outdoor gear for the person he thought he should be — the active outdoorsman, the prolific painter. He never got rid of any of it. The fantasy equipment stayed. He never questioned it. That's what the pattern looks like when nobody breaks it. The useful version — the one that applies to you — is that getting rid of objects that represent who you thought you'd be doesn't make you less of a person. It just frees you from managing who you aren't.

The Ripple Effect: How Decluttering Improves Everything Else

The benefits of decluttering extend beyond your physical environment. Living in an organized, functional space affects your habits, relationships, productivity, and general sense of well-being in ways that compound over time.

When your environment is organized, you make better decisions about what to bring into it. The one-in-one-out rule becomes easier to follow because you can see the impact of new acquisitions on your space. You become more selective about purchases because you're not shopping to fill emotional voids or to solve problems that don't exist.

The sense of control that comes from an organized environment is hard to describe until you've experienced it. When your environment is chaotic, you feel like you're constantly reacting. When it's organized, you feel like you're choosing. That shift is the real payoff of decluttering — not the clean surfaces, but the mental clarity that comes with them.

The changes that come after a major declutter tend to surprise people because they extend well beyond the obvious ones.

People report making better financial decisions. When your home isn't full of things you bought impulsively and regret, the pattern becomes visible. You can see what you actually use and enjoy versus what you acquired on automatic. That visibility changes buying behavior in ways that willpower never quite manages.

People report better relationships. Not because clutter is a relationship problem per se, but because the shame of a cluttered home causes social withdrawal — declining invitations to reciprocate, avoiding having people over, the low-level social avoidance that comes from not wanting anyone to see how you live. Remove the shame and the avoidance often goes with it.

People report more time. This one surprises them most. They hadn't thought of clutter as a time consumer. But cleaning a decluttered home takes a fraction of the time of cleaning a cluttered one. Finding things takes no time when things have places. The maintenance that felt like an endless burden becomes, in a decluttered home, a twenty-minute weekly task.

And people report — this is the one that's hardest to quantify but the most commonly mentioned — a sense of living more intentionally. When your home contains only things you chose to keep, everything in it is a choice. You stop being managed by your possessions and start managing them. That shift in relationship — from passive recipient of accumulated stuff to active curator of a chosen environment — is the real transformation.

Hosting and Socializing: Having Space for People Again

My friend Tasha had a spare bedroom that had been a dumping ground for seven years. She'd moved in, put some boxes in there "temporarily," and then the room had just accumulated whatever didn't have an obvious home elsewhere. By the time we talked about it, she couldn't see the floor. She'd stopped going in there. She called it "the room" with a particular tone of voice that meant the problem room, the room she was avoiding, the room she didn't want to deal with.

Her sister lived four hours away. They were close, but they hadn't seen each other in almost three years because Tasha had nowhere to put her. Her sister had two kids. A hotel was expensive. It just hadn't happened.

It took two weekends to clear the room. The boxes were mostly things that should have been donated or thrown away years earlier — not sentimental, not valuable, just stuff that had been easier to put in there than to make a decision about. Once we started going through it, almost nothing was hard to let go of. The difficulty had been starting, not the actual decisions.

She painted the room. Got a bed, a dresser, a lamp. Spent maybe three hundred dollars total. Within two months her sister came to visit with the kids, first time in nearly three years.

When I asked her later what had surprised her most about clearing the room, she said it wasn't the room itself. It was realizing how long she'd let a pile of boxes sit between her and seeing her sister. The clutter had felt like a private inconvenience. She hadn't thought of it as something that was costing her a relationship.

That's the thing about clutter that goes unexamined for years. It rarely costs you one big thing. It costs you small things, repeatedly, quietly, until you notice that some part of your life has been on hold.

One of the most significant changes that comes with decluttering is the ability to invite people into your space without embarrassment. Many people living in cluttered environments gradually become socially isolated because they're ashamed of their homes and don't want anyone to see how they're living.

When your space is functional and you're not embarrassed by it, the calculus around having people over changes. It stops being a source of anxiety and starts being a possibility. That's a meaningful quality of life shift that has nothing to do with minimalism and everything to do with having a home that works.

The experience of reclaimed physical space is something people consistently underestimate before they've had it.

Not the visual aspect — most people can imagine what a cleaner room looks like. The kinetic aspect. The way it feels to move through a room that isn't congested. The way your body responds differently to an uncluttered environment versus a cluttered one. The ease of finding things, of cleaning, of simply existing in a space that isn't working against you.

People who live in cluttered environments adapt to the congestion the way they adapt to background noise — they stop noticing it consciously, but their bodies are still navigating around it. Every time you reroute around a pile, every time you move something to get to something else, every time you visually scan a cluttered surface for the thing you need, your nervous system is registering the friction even when your conscious mind isn't.

Remove the friction and the relief is physical. People describe it as feeling lighter, as breathing more easily, as sleeping better in a bedroom that isn't doubling as storage. These aren't metaphors. They're accurate descriptions of what happens when your physical environment stops being an obstacle course.

The space you reclaim also tends to find uses you hadn't anticipated. The cleared dining room table becomes the place you actually eat meals together. The spare bedroom becomes the office or studio or guest room it was always supposed to be. The garage becomes a workshop or a place to park the car. The reclaimed space reveals possibilities that the clutter had obscured.

One of the more unexpected outcomes people report after decluttering is reconnecting with interests that had been buried — sometimes literally — under the accumulation.

The painting supplies that hadn't been touched in years because they were in a closet behind boxes. The guitar that hadn't been played because it was in a corner behind furniture. The sewing materials that hadn't been used because the workspace had been overtaken by things without homes.

When you clear the physical space, the psychological space often opens with it. The interest hadn't died — it had been crowded out by the management demands of a cluttered environment and the low-level guilt of owning things you weren't using. Remove the clutter and the interest re-emerges.

This is different from the aspirational objects discussed in Chapter 1 — the kayak for the outdoor life you never lived. The distinction is whether the interest was ever genuinely active. If you actually painted for years and then stopped because life got complicated, the supplies represent a real interest that may re-emerge when conditions change. If you bought the supplies because you wanted to become someone who painted, and you never actually did, the distinction is clearer.

Pay attention during the decluttering process to what you feel reluctant to let go of versus what you feel relieved to let go of. The things you feel genuinely reluctant about — not guilty, not obligated, but actually reluctant — may be pointing at something real that deserves a second look before it goes in the donate pile.

Rediscovering Hobbies and Interests

Clutter doesn't just take up physical space — it takes up mental and emotional space too. When you're constantly managing, organizing, and worrying about your stuff, there's less energy left for the activities and interests that bring you joy.

In my own case, decluttering freed up the mental bandwidth to actually pursue things I cared about instead of managing things I'd accumulated. The hobbies that survived the purges — the stamps I kept, the miniatures I paint, the photography I do — are the ones that actually mattered. Everything else was aspiration dressed up as identity.

The Unexpected Joy of Maintenance

This might sound crazy, but many people discover maintaining a decluttered space is enjoyable. When you have systems that work and everything has a designated place, putting things away becomes satisfying rather than overwhelming.

Cleaning a decluttered room takes minutes instead of hours. You're not moving piles of stuff around or trying to find places for things that don't belong anywhere. You're just returning items to their homes and wiping down clear surfaces.

The maintenance tasks become meditative rather than stressful. There's something deeply satisfying about putting things in order, seeing clear surfaces, and knowing where everything belongs. It's like the adult version of organizing your toys as a child - intrinsically rewarding even though it's technically work.

This is the difference between maintaining order and creating order. Maintaining order is straightforward and satisfying. Creating order from chaos is exhausting and overwhelming. Once you've done the hard work of decluttering, the ongoing maintenance is surprisingly pleasant.

There's a specific freedom that comes from living in a home where everything has been chosen rather than accumulated.

It's the freedom from the background guilt of things undone. Every cluttered space carries a small weight — the awareness that this needs to be dealt with, that you haven't gotten to it, that it represents something unresolved. A spare room full of boxes is a reminder, every time you walk past it, that you have a problem you haven't addressed. A closet so packed it doesn't close properly is a daily small frustration. A desk buried in papers is a constant visual signal of overwhelm.

When those things are resolved, the signals stop. The background noise quiets. This isn't a metaphor — it's a measurable reduction in the cognitive load your environment is imposing on you. The mental space that was occupied by undone things becomes available for things you actually care about.

What people do with that space varies enormously. Some take up projects they'd been putting off for years, now that the environment no longer feels like an obstacle. Some reconnect with hobbies that had been buried — literally, in some cases — under the accumulated weight of the previous life. Some simply find that their baseline mood has improved in ways they can't entirely attribute to any single change, but that coincide exactly with the clearing.

That's the real return on the work: not a clean aesthetic, but a clear mental environment. The work is worth doing for that reason alone.

The deepest thing a decluttered home gives you isn't a clean aesthetic. It's the experience of living in a space that's on your side.

Everything in your home, when the accumulation is gone, is something you chose. Something that serves you. Something that earns its place. Living in that kind of environment is different in a way that's hard to describe until you've had it — a baseline sense of control, of intention, of your home being an expression of your actual life rather than a record of your accumulated past.

That's what the title of this book means. Dead people don't need stuff because they're finished living. You're not. Make sure your home reflects that.

Living in the Present Instead of the Past

Perhaps the most profound change that comes with decluttering is the shift from living in the past to living in the present. Clutter is often a physical manifestation of psychological attachment to previous versions of yourself, old relationships, past interests, and expired dreams.

When you let go of the physical objects, you also let go of the psychological weight they were carrying. You stop being the curator of your own personal museum and start being the author of your current life.

Jerry never stopped defining himself by outdoor activities he'd always meant to pursue. Valerie never stopped keeping kitchen gadgets for the person she thought she should be. None of them broke the pattern. I did. That's the entire point of this book — not that the pattern is easy to break, but that it can be broken, and that recognition is the prerequisite. Without recognizing what the accumulation is actually doing, nothing else works.

Your house should serve your current life, not preserve evidence of every life you've ever lived. When you clear out the physical clutter, you make room for the life you're living right now. And that life, it turns out, is much more interesting than the museum of your abandoned dreams ever was.

Conclusion: Your Stuff Will Outlive You (Make Peace with That)

So here we are at the end. If you've been following along, you've learned some uncomfortable truths — about clutter, about the psychology behind it, and about how patterns established in childhood have a way of following you into your adult life whether you invite them or not.

You've learned that dead people don't need stuff. This isn't just a clever title designed to get your attention at the bookstore. This fundamental truth cuts through all the psychological barriers, emotional attachments, and elaborate justifications we create for keeping things we don't need.

When you die, someone else is going to go through your belongings and decide what to keep, what to donate, and what to throw away. They're going to make these decisions quickly, without the emotional attachments you spent decades building up, and they're going to judge your life based on what you left behind.

Do you really want to be remembered as the person who kept seventeen extension cords "just in case"? The person whose garage was so full of broken appliances that they had to park their car in the driveway for fifteen years? The person whose house was so cluttered that their family couldn't have people over for dinner?

The Legacy Question: What Do You Really Want to Leave Behind?

My parents never decluttered. Not once, not really. They tried once — pulled everything out of every room over a weekend, got overwhelmed, and shoved it all back. After that they stopped trying. The accumulation continued. And then they disappeared. For nearly a decade, nobody in the family could find them. No forwarding address, no phone calls, no contact. It turned out they had moved to a small subsidized apartment fifty miles away without telling anyone. They brought everything with them. When we finally learned where they were, the apartment was packed floor to ceiling. When my mother died, my father donated the contents of one storage unit. When my father died, I got a call from the social worker who managed the apartment complex. She described the scene and asked what to do. I told her to donate everything. That was the entirety of the estate settlement.

That's what the other path looks like. Not a dramatic ending. Not a cautionary tale with a tidy moral. Just a phone call to a social worker and a donation to strangers. Decades of accumulation, and the entire legacy fit in one phone call.

The thing is, my parents weren't incapable people. Jerry and Valerie ran Richard Lowe's Gallery of Wildlife Art in Lake Arrowhead, California. They built a business. They raised a family. They were smart, creative people who had skills and drive. The destitution wasn't inevitable. It was the accumulated result of decades of decisions — about money, about stuff, about what mattered. That was part of their legacy too.

Here's what I've come to believe: what you leave behind is part of who you were. You're dead, so you could argue it doesn't matter. But it matters to the people who loved you. Your family, your friends, the communities you were part of — they're going to go through your things. Everyone does. And what they find shapes the last version of you they carry around in their heads.

Do you want them to find mountains of old decayed magazines going back half a century? Boxes of things that were too good to throw away but never good enough to use? Every secret you kept, every embarrassment you meant to get rid of? Because that's what they'll find if you don't decide.

Or would you rather they found the things that actually represent you? For me, that means clean, organized rooms. Models I built. Photographs I took. Books I actually read. Fantasy miniatures I painted. Things that say: this is who I am, this is what I care about, this is how I spend my time. Not a warehouse of regret, but a record of a life.

That's the legacy question. Not what you want to leave to people in a legal sense, but what picture of yourself you want to leave behind. Every item you clear out now is one less thing that misrepresents you later. Every collection you curate, every shelf you organize, every drawer you actually deal with — that's you choosing how you'll be remembered.

I chose a different path than my parents. Not all at once, and not easily. I watched my mother's depression get temporarily soothed by purchases and absorbed that as a coping mechanism without realizing it. After I moved out, I spent vast sums on junk trying to solve problems that buying couldn't solve. Board games to fix loneliness. Equipment for hobbies I never pursued. Computers, cameras, costumes. A full moving van every time I relocated. Debt. More depression. A spiral. I recognized it, eventually. That recognition made all the difference. I learned to distinguish between what was genuinely mine and what was just accumulated. They never did.

One of the biggest barriers to decluttering is the guilt people feel about getting rid of items that belonged to deceased relatives. I've seen people keep entire houses full of their parents' belongings for years after they died, turning their own homes into museums dedicated to people who can no longer enjoy or benefit from the preservation.

Your dead relatives want you to know: they don't care about their stuff anymore. They're dead. They have moved beyond material possessions and into whatever comes after life, whether that's heaven, reincarnation, or just nothing at all.

Your grandmother doesn't care if you keep her china set. She's not watching from beyond the grave, keeping score of which grandchildren honor her memory by storing her belongings properly. She would rather you be happy and live in a functional house than turn yourself into the unpaid curator of her personal museum.

Katherine and Justin, Jerry's parents, died before I was old enough to know them well. Their belongings were distributed among Jerry, Valerie, and various relatives. Jerry kept some of his father's tools for years — not because he used them, but because getting rid of them felt like discarding Justin. The tools stayed. Jerry died. The tools stayed some more. Nobody ever did anything with them. That is a completely normal outcome and not a failure. The point isn't that inherited objects must be released. The point is that keeping them out of guilt rather than love isn't honoring anyone. It's just adding weight.

The same principle applies to all inherited items. The best way to honor someone's memory is to live your own life fully, not to turn your house into a storage facility for their possessions. Keep the items that genuinely bring you joy or serve a practical purpose in your life. Let go of everything else with gratitude for the person who owned it, but without guilt about choosing your current life over their past one.

Most people who read a book like this fall into one of three categories.

The first group reads it and starts immediately. The resistance is low or they're at a point of genuine crisis with their space, and the combination of recognition and practical framework is enough to get them moving. These are the people who email authors to say they cleared their garage the weekend after finishing the last chapter.

The second group reads it, feels genuinely motivated, and then doesn't start for weeks or months. The motivation was real but it dissipated before it converted to action. These people often need to re-read the early chapters — specifically the sections on what accumulation is actually costing them — to reconnect with why the work matters.

The third group reads it and recognizes that they're not quite ready. The accumulation is tied to something — grief, depression, anxiety, a life situation that hasn't resolved yet — and the timing isn't right. These people often come back to it six months or two years later, when the underlying thing has shifted enough that the practical work becomes possible.

All three of these are fine. There is no wrong timeline. The only thing that doesn't work is reading a book like this, feeling the recognition, and then deciding that recognition is the same thing as change. It isn't. Recognition is the prerequisite. The work still has to happen.

Wherever you are in this process — ready to start, not quite ready, somewhere in the middle of it already — the most important thing is honesty about where you actually are. From there, the next step is always clear, even if it's not the step you were hoping for.

Celebrating Small Wins: Every Cleared Surface is a Victory

Decluttering doesn't have to be an all-or-nothing transformation that happens overnight. Some people need months or even years to work through decades of accumulated possessions, and that's fine. The goal isn't to become a minimalist overnight, it's to create a living space that serves your current life instead of preserving your entire history.

Every small step counts. Every cleared surface is a victory. Every item you donate is a decision to choose your future over your past. Every system you implement to prevent re-accumulation is an investment in your ongoing sanity and happiness.

The turning point for me wasn't a single dramatic purge. It was recognizing the pattern. Seeing that the buying wasn't helping — that it was creating debt and making the depression worse, not better. Once I saw it, I couldn't unsee it. That recognition was the prerequisite to everything else. No decluttering method works until you understand why you're accumulating in the first place.

Celebrate progress instead of focusing on how much work remains. If you cleared off your kitchen counter today, that's worth celebrating even if your garage still looks like a tornado hit a thrift store. If you donated a bag of clothes you don't wear, that's progress even if your closet is still overcrowded.

Start where you are, with what you have, and celebrate every step forward. Decluttering is a skill that improves with practice, and every decision to let go of something you don't need makes the next decision easier.

The Ongoing Journey: Decluttering is a Lifestyle, Not a Destination

Decluttering isn't a project you complete once and then forget about. It's a way of living that requires ongoing attention and conscious decision-making about what you allow into your life and what you choose to keep.

Consumer culture is designed to undermine your decluttering efforts. Companies spend billions of dollars convincing you that you need things you don't need, that buying something will solve problems you don't have, and that accumulating possessions will make you happier, more successful, or more attractive.

Every advertisement you see, every promotional email you receive, every "limited time offer" you encounter is part of a coordinated effort to turn you back into a consumer who buys first and thinks later. The forces trying to fill your house with clutter are organized, well-funded, and relentless.

Your defense against this assault on your peace of mind is equally simple and revolutionary: conscious decision-making about everything that enters your life. Ask yourself whether you need something before you buy it. Question whether new possessions will genuinely improve your life or just add to your maintenance burden. Choose experiences over objects, relationships over acquisitions, and contentment over consumption.

This doesn't mean you can never buy anything or that you have to live like a monk in an empty room. It means being intentional about your choices instead of automatic. It means understanding the true cost of ownership: not just the purchase price but the time, space, and mental energy required to maintain everything you own.

Your defense doesn't require willpower or asceticism. It just requires the habit of asking one question before anything enters your home: does this deserve space in my life? That question, asked consistently, does more work than any organizational system ever will.

The ongoing practice of conscious living is more satisfying than the temporary high of acquiring new possessions. When you choose quality over quantity, intention over impulse, and contentment over consumption, you discover that you need much less than you thought to be happy.

Living Authentically in the Present

The deepest benefit of decluttering isn't having a clean house or being able to find your keys when you need them, although those things are nice. The deepest benefit is the freedom to live authentically in the present instead of being weighed down by the accumulated evidence of every person you've ever been or thought you might become.

Decluttering allows you to stop being the curator of your own personal history museum and start being the author of your current life. When you let go of the exercise equipment for the athletic person you never became, you make space for activities you enjoy. When you donate the hobby supplies for the crafty person you thought you should be, you free up time and energy for interests that genuinely engage you.

For me, it meant going from a three-bedroom apartment with fifteen bookshelves layered with books, movies, and equipment for a dozen abandoned hobbies, to a home with seven organized bookshelves and space to actually move through. Half a dozen purge campaigns over the years. Each one teaching something the last one didn't. The stamps I kept are the ones I genuinely care about. The books I kept are the ones I actually read. What's left is mine — not aspirational, not compensatory, not inherited anxiety. Just the things that belong in my life.

The things that survive your honest purges are the things that are actually you. Everything else was noise. Comfortable, familiar noise — but noise.

What to Do in the Next 24 Hours

Before you close this book and let it become part of your clutter, do one thing. Go find your junk drawer. Spend twenty minutes. Throw out everything that is obviously junk. That's it. One drawer, twenty minutes. Let that be the first evidence that this works.

In the next week, run the Emotional Audit on one small category — a shelf, a box, a drawer that isn't the junk drawer. Ask the questions in the Emotional Audit about each object. Notice which ones produce the low hum of bad feeling when you hold them. Those go first.

In the next month, work through one full room using whatever method in Chapter 2 suited your personality. Use the four piles. Make the decisions. Get comfortable with the process.

Over the next year, run at least two full decluttering campaigns. Not necessarily massive purges — a weekend each, or a series of focused sessions. The goal is to make it a recurring practice rather than a crisis response. People who declutter regularly never have to excavate. They maintain.

And keep asking the question that cuts through everything else: does this still have value in my life right now? Not in the past, not in some hypothetical future. Right now. The answer is usually faster than you expect.

The practical reality of decluttering is that most people do it wrong at the start. They try to do too much at once, run out of energy, end up with everything pulled out of the closets and spread across the floor, and shove it all back in because they've run out of time or motivation. They declare it impossible and don't try again for years.

If that's your history with this, it doesn't mean you failed. It means you used the wrong approach.

The right approach is smaller and more patient than the dramatic transformation suggests. One drawer. One shelf. One afternoon. Not one house, one weekend. Sustainable progress accumulates faster than you'd expect when it doesn't deplete you.

Here's what a realistic first month looks like: Week one, the junk drawer. Week two, one closet shelf. Week three, under one bed. Week four, one bathroom cabinet. That's it. Four sessions, probably two hours total. At the end of the month, four spaces in your home are genuinely better. That's real progress. That builds momentum. That teaches you the process without burning you out.

By month three, the pace picks up because you've built the muscle. Decisions come faster. The donate bag is a habit. The rescue reflex is familiar enough that you recognize it and don't obey it automatically. The whole thing starts to feel like something you can actually finish, which is a feeling that was never available when you were trying to do everything at once.

Celebrate the cleared drawer. Celebrate the closet you can actually navigate. Celebrate the box that went to Goodwill. These aren't small things dressed up as victories. They are victories. The sum of them is a different kind of home and a different relationship with your stuff — which is what this was always about.

The forces working against a decluttered home are real and worth understanding clearly.

Consumer culture is not a background condition. It's an active system that is extremely good at what it does. Every advertisement is an argument for acquisition. Every sale creates artificial urgency. Every product is designed to seem like a solution to a problem you may not have had before you saw it. Retail environments are engineered to maximize purchases through lighting, placement, and the social proof of other people buying things.

None of this is conspiracy. It's just business. But understanding it changes your relationship to shopping. You're not making neutral choices in a neutral environment. You're making choices inside a system that has invested enormous resources in getting you to buy things, and the default outcome of that system — absent any active resistance on your part — is accumulation.

The active resistance isn't complicated. It's the habit of asking one question before any acquisition: does this deserve space in my life? Not "do I want this," which is a question the consumer system is extremely good at producing a yes answer to. Not "is this a good price," which is an argument about value that sidesteps whether you need the thing at all. Does this deserve space in my life — the finite, irreplaceable space of your home and your attention and your time.

That question, asked consistently, does more to maintain a decluttered home than any organizational system ever invented.

The other active resistance is periodic reassessment. Every year, things that were true about your life stop being true. Interests change. Circumstances change. The person you were when you bought something may no longer be the person you are. The annual purge isn't just about catching accumulation. It's about ensuring your home continues to reflect your actual current life rather than an outdated version of it.

Here's the honest version of what you can expect.

The first session will be harder than subsequent ones. You'll question whether you're making the right decisions, whether you're keeping too much or letting go of too much, whether you should be doing this differently. This is normal. Push through it.

By the third or fourth session, the decisions come faster. You've built a vocabulary for the process — you know what keep feels like, what donate feels like, what the rescue reflex feels like when it appears. The friction is lower.

Somewhere in the process, you'll hit something hard. A box of a deceased relative's things. Objects from a relationship that ended painfully. A category that represents a version of yourself you haven't fully let go of. When you hit it, don't force it. Set it aside, come back to it when you're more ready, and continue with the easier material. The hard stuff doesn't have to be done first. It just has to be done eventually.

After the first major declutter, the maintenance is genuinely easier than the initial work. Not effortless, but manageable. The monthly check takes an hour. The annual review takes a weekend. Neither feels like the grinding labor of the first pass through years of accumulated stuff.

The results are real. Not the magazine-worthy transformation of a professional staging — your home will still look like your home. But a version of your home where you can find things, where you're not embarrassed to have people in, where the visual noise has dropped to a level where you can actually see what you own and appreciate it.

That's what you're working toward. It's worth the work to get there.

The Final Word: Choose Your Life Over Your Stuff

If you take only one thing away from this book, let it be this: your stuff should serve your life, not control it. Every item you own should earn its place in your house by contributing to your happiness, productivity, or well-being. If something isn't making your life better, it's making your life worse.

You have a choice about how you want to live. You can continue accumulating possessions in the hope that the right combination of objects will finally make you feel successful, prepared, or complete. Or you can recognize that contentment comes from living intentionally with less rather than automatically with more.

Dead people don't need stuff, but living people need space: physical space to move around comfortably, mental space to think clearly, and emotional space to focus on what matters. When you clear out the clutter, you make room for the life you want to live instead of preserving evidence of all the lives you've already lived.

My parents showed me what the alternative looks like. Jerry and Valerie accumulated until they couldn't anymore, disappeared into a subsidized apartment nobody knew about, and died in it. I saw the pattern early enough to do something about it. That's the only difference between their story and mine — not talent, not willpower, just recognition.

You are a living person with choices to make about how you want to spend your time, energy, and attention. Choose wisely. Choose consciously. Choose your life over your stuff, your present over your past, and your authentic self over the versions of yourself that exist only in the objects you've accumulated.

Make peace with the fact that your stuff will outlive you, but make sure your life is more memorable than your belongings. Live in a way that honors the person you are right now instead of preserving monuments to every person you've ever been.

The people who make lasting changes to their relationship with stuff share one characteristic: they understood why they were doing it before they started.

Not "I want a cleaner house." That's too abstract to sustain the work when it gets hard. Something more specific. Something connected to daily life in a way that matters to them personally.

Some of them wanted to be able to have their grandchildren over without embarrassment. Some wanted to stop spending money on storage units. Some wanted to reclaim a room that had been unusable for years. Some had watched a parent or relative's accumulation become a crisis and were determined not to repeat it. Some had gone through the process of settling an estate and decided, standing in a house full of things that had to be sorted by strangers, that they wanted to leave something different behind.

Whatever the reason, the ones who sustain it are the ones who can articulate it clearly — who know what they're working toward in terms concrete enough to return to when the process feels endless.

You've read this book. You know how the psychology works, what the practical methods are, how maintenance operates, what life looks like on the other side. What you need now is the specific answer to the specific question: what changes when you're done?

Find that answer. Hold onto it. Start with the junk drawer.

Everything else follows from there

About the Author

Richard Lowe grew up in a hoarding household, spent his twenties and thirties replicating the patterns he observed there, and eventually figured out how to stop. He is not a therapist. He is a person who has executed seven major decluttering campaigns, owns his collections with full awareness of what they are, and has reduced fifteen layered bookshelves to seven organized ones over the course of several years of genuinely uncomfortable self-examination.

He once spent an entire $2,000 gift card on board games to solve a loneliness problem. He kept a camera setup worth $4,000 that he rarely used because getting rid of it would mean admitting the portrait and wedding business hadn't materialized. He owned a MicroVAX. He has thrown out things that made him feel better for a week and kept things he should have thrown out years earlier. He has made every mistake in this book at least once, which is why he was able to write it.

Professionally, Richard spent twenty years as Director of Computer Operations at Trader Joe's, managing technology for a $16 billion company. He has published 113+ books on subjects ranging from cybersecurity to decluttering to fiction, and works as a ghostwriter for executives and entrepreneurs who have a story to tell but not the time or inclination to write it. He has documented 950,000+ photographs across renaissance festivals, masquerade balls, and bellydance communities.

He currently maintains curated collections of Tonga stamps, Disney stamps, Tournament of Roses pins, and painted miniatures. The key word is curated. He knows where all of it is. None of it is in a storage unit he hasn't opened in three years. None of it is carrying emotional weight he doesn't want to live with.

You can find his other books at masterofworlds.com and his ghostwriting services at thewritingking.com. He promises the website is better organized than his mother's apartment was.

Books by Richard Lowe

See books by Richard Lowe at
https://masterofworlds.com

Get free publishing insights and industry updates at
https://thewritingking.substack.com

For ghostwriting and book coaching services see
https://thewritingking.com

www.ingramcontent.com/pod-product-compliance
Lightning Source LLC
Chambersburg PA
CBHW032034050726
47590CB00006B/2405